THE LORD'S PRAYERS

The Lord's Prayers

By

Elton Trueblood
Professor of Philosophy
Earlham College

HARPER & ROW, PUBLISHERS

NEW YORK, EVANSTON, AND LONDON

The quotations from the Bible which appear in this volume are from the Revised Standard Version, unless otherwise noted.

FIRST EDITION

LIBRARY OF CONGRESS CATALOG CARD NUMBER: 65-10706

L-O

TO
ARNOLD ELTON TRUEBLOOD

Contents

Contents

Preface

Most of us admit that our days are radically unequal. On some days we accomplish more or understand more than we understand or accomplish in entire months, under less favorable circumstances. There are dull days, when we see very little, but there are also some which Rufus Jones loved to call days of high visibility. Such a day came to me in March, 1964, when I was worshiping with the noonday congregation of St. Paul's Church, in Richmond, Virginia.

Having promised to give a series of talks for the week, a set of addresses had been prepared, but suddenly, on Monday noon, an entirely different series came to me. I realized, more keenly than ever before, how inept it is to speak of the Lord's Prayer, since we were all aware of more than one in the Gospels, and also since the "Our Father" was primarily intended for the followers rather than for the Leader. The possibility of the plural appealed to me strongly and I decided to announce a series on The Lord's Prayers.

The series was given to the St. Paul's weekday congregation and the experience of giving the separate talks was, to me, a minor revelation. Soon I saw that the theme had a universal application and therefore ought not to be limited to a single company. Consequently, I determined to put my meditations on this important theme into book form and now a number of weeks, mostly alone in the wilderness, have made the writing possible. I hope the effort to become acquainted with a basic segment of Christ's life will be as rewarding to my readers as it has been to me.

E. T.

Pen Point
Greentown, Pennsylvania
August, 1964

CHAPTER I

❧❧❧

Creative Imitation

> "Lord, teach us to pray, as John
> taught his disciples."
> *Luke* 11:1

A CHRISTIAN IS ONE who tries to follow Christ. The trenchant command "Follow me" appears at the beginning of the Gospel and it appears, likewise, at the end. The first injunction of Christ, according to Mark's account, was to Simon and Andrew, "Follow me and I will make you become fishers of men" (1:17), while, according to John, His last words were those addressed to Peter, ". . . what is that to you? Follow me!" (21:22). Therefore, it is not surprising that whenever we try to emphasize deeds more than words, the theme of Christian imitation is dominant. This is not all that there is to the Christian life, but it appears again and again. We read, for example, in John 12:26, "If any one serves me, he must follow me." Above all, this is a magnificent point at which to begin, for it launches the new Christian with a joint sense of humility and grandeur.

The most famous of all treatments of the theme is the Latin work associated with the name of Thomas à Kempis and assembled in the lower Rhineland. *The Imitation of Christ* first appeared anonymously in 1418 and has exerted a continuous influence for nearly five and a half centuries. The evidence of its appeal is seen in the fact that it has been translated into more than fifty languages, and next to the Bible, is the most influential book of Christendom.[1] The opening line of the book is really a quotation from Christ, as found in John 8:12: "He who follows me will not walk in darkness."

The words of Christ, says *The Imitation*, admonish us "to imitate His life and example, if we would be truly enlightened and delivered from all blindness of heart." This conception arises, not from any optimistic judgment about natural human goodness, but rather from a realistic estimate of human need. We have need to follow Him precisely because our life otherwise is innately impoverished. The golden text of *The Imitation* is expressed memorably as follows: "Therefore let our foremost resolve be to meditate upon the Life of Jesus Christ." The idea is that such repeated meditation tends to become determinative in the structure of our own feeble souls. "Meditate on His life," says the famous book, "and thou wilt be ashamed to find how far removed thou art from His perfection." Continuous confrontation emphasizes, by consequence, both our unworthiness and our hope, both our separation from God and our potential reconciliation with Him.

The theme of imitation, though associated in the popular mind with à Kempis and the Brothers and Sisters of the Common Life, is by no means limited to the fifteenth century. The tradition is represented by such different leaders as Ignatius at the end of the first century A.D., William Penn in the seventeenth century, and William Law in the eighteenth.[2]

Because there are many aspects of Christ's life which we

[1] The best contemporary edition is that of William Collins Sons and Company, London and Glasgow, 1957. This edition presents a new English translation by George F. Maine.

[2] G. McLeod Bryan has collected in one volume the sayings of thirty-nine Christian writers, in many centuries, on the imitation theme. The book is published with the title, *In His Likeness* (London: Society for the Promotion of Christian Knowledge, 1961). The anthology is graced by a Foreword by the late H. Richard Niebuhr who writes, "There are those Jesus Christ calls upon to imitate Him as a child imitates a parent; those others whom He sets to work to copy His words and deeds; and still others who, like advanced apprentices, are being taught to be and to do an independent work that is in the spirit of the Master Workman."

may seek deliberately to imitate, we are likely to be more nearly successful if we concentrate upon one of these at a time. Thus we may meditate upon His compassion, upon His humor, upon His method of teaching by parables, etc. If we are especially concerned for the development of our inner lives, we can do no better than to concentrate upon His prayers. That is the sole reason for this particular book.

As we immerse our minds in the Gospels, we are continually surprised at what we find in them. Words which we have seen a dozen times, without their having any sharp impact, suddenly disturb us on the next careful reading. This has happened to a good many persons as they have sought to isolate the subject of prayer. We are amazed to see how pervasive the subject is. We soon note, of course, at least three aspects of the theme. First, there is Christ's teaching *about* prayer; second, there is much reference, by the authors or editors, to the fact that Christ prayed on various occasions; and, third, there is the record, in more or less fragmentary form, of the actual prayers uttered by Christ. As we look at this body of material we know that we are dealing, not with something peripheral, but with something intrinsic to the spiritual life of man.

Of all the parts of the Gospel record, there is no part of greater practical significance for us than that which relates to prayer. Christ confronts us in His parables, in His laughter, and in His suffering, but the deepest confronting comes when we meet our Lord at prayer. Here is an antidote to all that is superficial in religion; here is an alternative to cheap grace. Here is the religion of experience which is also evangelical in the sense that it is Christ-centered.

The more we reflect, the more we realize that prayer is the heart of genuine religion. If this were well understood there would be no need to speak of "religionless Christianity." Basic to private religion is private prayer, and basic to public religion is public prayer. All who think with any clarity understand that prayer is far more than any mere verbal form. Prayer is an experience of pure trust and loving obedience which elevates even a modest life when truly related to the Living God. Prayer, in this sense, is nothing of which we need to be ashamed, intellectually or in any other way. George Buttrick has been extremely helpful at this point. He says, "To dismiss the universal fact of prayer as 'projection' is not impressive; the tiny psychological cliché is not big enough to cover the age-long plea."[3]

The cynic who scoffs at prayer, thinking that he can dismiss it, becomes particularly ridiculous when it is Christ's practice of prayer at which he scoffs. If Christ was wrong at this point He was wrong absolutely. Only the very arrogant are willing to go out on that limb. I know I may be deluded in *my* prayers, but I refuse to make the monstrous judgment that He was deluded in *His*.

Surprisingly few books have been written about Christ's prayers.[4] Usually the references to the tremendous fact that Christ prayed are brief and incidental to some other purpose. A good illustration of this approach is in Harry Emerson Fosdick's remarkable little book, *The Manhood of the Master*, which had such an impact upon earlier student generations. In the light of Dr. Fosdick's intention of bringing out the human side of Christ's nature, it is really surprising that he did not include an entire chapter on Christ at prayer. Instead, he gave us only about a page, but it was an extremely helpful page. "The Master," he wrote, "prayed as naturally as a child breathes."[5] This was more valuable to his readers than many pages of tortured prose might have been. It took a person of Dr. Fosdick's unusual insight to see that the only thing which

[3] The sentence quoted from Dr. Buttrick appeared first in a sermon in Memorial Church at Harvard University. See *Sermons Preached in a University Church* (Nashville: Abingdon Press, 1959), p. 16.

[4] Among books in print in English the most helpful are James G. S. S. Thomson, *The Praying Christ* (Grand Rapids: Wm. B. Eerdman's Publishing Co., 1959), and Ralph S. Cushman, *The Prayers of Jesus* (Nashville: Abingdon Press, 1956). Bishop Cushman's book treats chiefly the so-called High Priestly Prayer and deals with all in a frankly devotional mood. He adds prayers and poems of his own.

[5] Harry Emerson Fosdick, *The Manhood of the Master* (New York: Association Press, 1913), p. 155.

the disciples are reported to have asked the Master to teach them was "how to pray."

When we reflect upon the matter in any depth, we soon see that the relative neglect of Christ's experience of prayer is not really surprising. After all, the whole matter is one of tremendous paradox. The fact that Christ prayed, one of the least doubtful in the entire record, is a standing challenge to all simple conceptions of who He was. The fact that Christ prayed, demonstrating thereby both personal humility and a sense of need, is hard for some people to make consistent with their interpretation of His divinity. How grateful we must be to the writers of the Gospels, who, in spite of their strong conviction that He was indeed the expected Messiah, did not fear to include in their narrative elements which might appear to be embarrassing. Mark, presumably the earliest of our authors, begins his account of Christ's public career with a condensed depiction of the three major elements in His ministry. First, He proclaimed a message remarkable for its mood and tense: "The time is fulfilled." Second, He called individual men. His Kingdom began to be a reality by the recruitment of men and women, one by one. Third, He *healed!* His work is distorted when we see Him in only one role. He was Teacher, Leader, and Healer and He was all three at the same time. The pattern, Mark would have us understand, began very early and was repeated on many subsequent occasions.

It is immediately following the Marcan description of this rapid threefold ministry that we get the first overt reference to Christ's prayer. "And in the morning, a great while before day, he rose and went out to a lonely place, and there he prayed" (Mark 1:35). Thus, very early, we find the statement of the paradox. Christ claimed, we must remember, that He was the true revelation of the Father. He could say, immediately after a prayer, "All things have been delivered to me by my Father; and no one knows the Son except the Father, and no one knows the Father except the Son and any one to whom the Son chooses to reveal him" (Matt. 11:27). Even more striking

are the words of the dialogue with the leaders of the Sanhe-
drin, "Again the high priest asked him, 'Are you the Christ,
the Son of the Blessed?' And Jesus said, 'I am . . .'" (Mark
14:61-62).

This is what Christians mean by saying that Christ was
divine. The earliest followers found something in Him which
they did not find in themselves. Simon and the others at
Caesarea Philippi realized, in a sudden burst of insight, that
He was "the Christ, the Son of the living God" (Matt. 16:16).
It is this aspect of Christ's life which has found expression in
the classic creeds of Christendom. The Apostles' Creed begins
by reference to both the Father and the Son: "I believe in God
the Father Almighty, Maker of heaven and earth: And in
Jesus Christ his only Son our Lord." In the Nicene Creed the
second phrase is greatly expanded and made much more ex-
plicit than it is in the Apostles' Creed: "And in one Lord
Jesus Christ, the only-begotten Son of God; Begotten of his
Father before all worlds, God of God, Light of Light, Very
God of very God."

The problem of uniting such expressions with the fact that
Jesus prayed is obvious. If Christ prayed to God, it is clear that
it is a heresy to say He *was* God. It would be meaningless to
pray to Himself. In fact, His prayers make it very clear that He
was praying to the Father, which is another way of saying that
He was *not* the Father. The clearest of Christ's denials of
identity is that of John 14:28, "The Father is greater than I."
He could say "I and the Father are one" (John 10:30), but
only a person unfamiliar with the ambiguity of the verb "to
be" would conclude from this that the relation involved is that
of identity. A good husband may say that he and his wife are
one, but this is no denial of separate individuality; it merely
refers to common purposes or the appreciation of common
values. Like almost everything that Christ said, the reference
to oneness is clearly figurative. When He said "I am the Good
Shepherd," it does not follow that He carried a crook, or that
when He said "I am the door," He was made of wood.

The central paradox about Christ is that He was both divine and human. Sometimes one side of this paradox needs to be stressed and sometimes the other. The central conviction is that what is clearly paradoxical is not necessarily inconsistent. To say that Jesus was a man of sorrows does not, by any stretch of logic, mean that He was not also a man of joys. We know that He wept, but there is, at the same time, abundant evidence that He laughed.

If Christ had not felt the need to pray, He might seem to us, especially in the light of His sinlessness, an impressive and awesome figure, but He would not seem close to our common lives. We need to pray, and He means more to us because He, too, needed to pray. We are not as close to the Father as He was, but we address the same Father. With Him, as with us, there was the need to learn to accept the Father's will. This is the clear meaning of the tremendous words, "Nevertheless, not as I will, but as thou wilt" (Matt. 26:39). One of the chief reasons for prayer is the fact of temptation, and Christ, we know, was tempted. To deny the reality of the temptations is to substitute a dogma for a known fact, the very essence of failure in intellectual integrity. Because Christ knew what it was to be tempted, He also knew how great the need of prayer was.

It is precisely because Christ, in His felt need of prayer, is close to us that the concept of imitation, as expressed by à Kempis and so many more, is truly relevant. It is not fully relevant in the sense that we can expect to be sinless as He was sinless. We certainly cannot copy Him in everything, for He was the express image of the Father in a way in which we are not. Because we are in the finite predicament, it will be necessary for us, over and over, to pray, "Forgive us our sins" (Luke 11:4). It is important to note that this phrase is not in one of Christ's own prayers, but in the suggested prayer for His followers. There is no reason to suppose that we shall ever, in this life, outgrow the appropriateness of this petition.

The obedience theme, valuable as it is, is like other valuable themes in that it involves its own particular dangers. The chief danger, in this instance, is that of oversimplicity. Simple obedience might require us to give to every beggar, even if we are fully assured that the beggar will immediately use our gift for alcohol and thus make himself worse. This very doubtful kindness seems to follow from literal obedience to "give to him who begs from you, and do not refuse him who would borrow from you" (Matt. 5:42). The problem is that the Gospel involves other values, such as a real concern for the beggar's welfare, and frequently the various values are in conflict. The simple answers are almost always wrong because they tend to neglect the element of paradox. Many of our moral problems arise, not because we lack principles, but because we recognize so *many* principles, and frequently they seem to be in direct conflict with one another.

To imitate everything about Christ would lead to absurdity and ultimately to a denial of Christ. There is, for example, no need to suppose that we must remain unmarried just because He was single, nor that we must observe various Judaic laws which He undoubtedly obeyed. We do not need to dress as He dressed nor to speak the language which He spoke. It may be a useful procedure to ask, in various situations, as Charles Sheldon asked, "What would Jesus do?" but the plain truth is that there are countless contemporary problems in which we have no idea what He would do. Would He accept the military draft? We do not know, because He gave neither precept nor example on this question, and, if we try to answer by reference to general principles, we find a variety of them. Does such a question relate to God primarily or to Caesar primarily? We do not know. Similarly, we do not know what He would do about voting in an election, particularly when there are features of both contending parties which we cannot approve. Perhaps He would say that there is one thing worse than imperfect voting, i.e., not voting at all. We do not know!

However unsatisfactory it is to try to imitate Christ in particular deeds, or to appeal to His practice in making concrete decisions, we do not find the same difficulty when we turn to prayer. Prayer is potentially so nearly universal that classic models are truly relevant. The language, for example, makes no difference. There is no hindrance in the supposed fact that Christ prayed in Aramaic, whereas we pray in English or in German or in French. Prayer is one form of speech which loses very little in translation. It is, furthermore, unimportant whether the prayer is uttered kneeling or standing, with the eyes open or closed, or even whether it is vocal or silent. Even the name by which the Living God is addressed makes no significant difference. There is no reason to suppose that the prayer of Socrates, at the end of the *Phaedrus*, was any less genuine because the Athenian used a Greek name. If the follower of Islam says "Allah" with sincerity and with reverence, there is no reason to conclude that God is displeased. The Eternal Father is no respecter of nomenclature!

The purpose of life is not only to live well, but also to live better. Almost any job that can be done at all can be improved. In the struggle to live better, ordinary mortals are greatly in need of determination, but they are also in need of a standard. Unworthy themselves, and often conscious of their unworthiness, they have the amazing ability of attaching their lives to something which is better than themselves. Herein lies much of the paradox of the greatness and the littleness of man; small we undoubtedly are, but we are made with the capacity for attachment to greatness. In even the dullest of us there is some latent ability to recognize the sublime and to be moved by it. Classics are those creations in which some recognition of greatness comes to the millions who, while not themselves capable of producing greatness, are nevertheless capable of its recognition. The lifting power of such creations is immense.

It is a major cultural fact that, by virtue of the permanence of the written word, some vision of greatness is afforded to succeeding generations, provided they are willing to listen. Some of the grandest passages of the Homeric poems reach us as truly today as they reached the Greeks who first encountered them, and the words of Shakespeare have not lost their explosive power in nearly four hundred years. It is by returning continually to such enduring resources that the tendency to accept contemporary triviality is repeatedly challenged. That this is true was understood and brilliantly stated by Longinus, whose famous fragment *On the Sublime* was apparently written near the beginning of the Christian Era. In a striking passage Longinus wrote:

Thus from the surpassing genius of the ancients, as from sacred outlets (one might say), channels run to the souls of those who emulate them, whereby even those not greatly susceptible to divine frenzy become inspired and participate in the grandeur of others. . . . This is not plagiarism, but like taking the impression of a fair form in sculpture or some other kind of art.[6]

What Longinus said long ago has been accepted by so many generations of thoughtful scholars that it is not seriously in doubt. The ideas of the Greek rhetorician, continuing, as they did, some of the basic insights of Aristotle, have become part of the enduring structure of Western thought. They help us to return again and again to *megethos*, i.e., to bigness, to amplitude, to importance. We seek the sublime, as contrasted with the trivial, and we soon learn that it is found in elevation.

The wisdom which we have inherited and which received its classic formulation in the words of Longinus, concerns a certain conception of imitation. The imitation and emulation of the acknowledged masters of past generations is a path leading to the sublime. These acknowledged masters are no longer on trial; their place is secure, and, indeed, far more secure than is any contemporary doctrine or scientific theory. The imitation of great style does not necessarily lead to slavishness, but may be a truly liberating experience.

By enormous good fortune there has been preserved for us, through all the tumultuous intervening years, an excellent

[6] Longinus, *On the Sublime*, English translation by Benedict Einarson (Chicago: Packard and Company, 1945), pp. 29, 30.

though incomplete record of how Jesus Christ lived and taught
and died and rose again. This has been set down in four little
books, called Gospels, written from four different points of
view. Each of the ancient authors supplements the others.[7] We
have reason to be glad that the four accounts are not carbon
copies of one another. Because Christ's basic message is approached from different and complementary angles, we have
something of a dialogue. These four books have been subjected
to more sustained and painstaking scholarly examination than
any other body of literature in the world.

We find in Matthew's Gospel the most succinct statement
of Christ's teaching about prayer, in a passage which deals with
two problems, the problem of solitude and the problem of
words. The first of these problems concerns the tendency to
make prayer a means of impressing other people, rather than
a genuine conversation with God, in which our entire interest
is in Him. Christ's brief statement is as follows:

"And when you pray, you must not be like the hypocrites; for
they love to stand and pray in the synagogues and at street corners,
that they may be seen by men. Truly I say to you, they have their
reward. But when you pray, go into your room and shut the door
and pray to your Father who is in secret; and your Father who sees
in secret will reward you." [Matt. 6:5-6]

One result of the tendency to take Biblical passages in isolation is the conclusion, often voiced, that it is wrong to pray
with others. If the above passage were all that Christ ever said
or demonstrated about prayer, such an extreme conclusion
might be justified, but the passage cannot bear the whole
weight of the problem, for there are others. For one thing, it
is clear that Christ Himself did not always go into His own
room to pray. He seems to have prayed everywhere, sometimes
alone and sometimes in a fellowship. That He did not always

[7] For a careful study of the different purposes of the authors of the different
Gospels see Wayne G. Rollins, *The Gospels: Portraits of Christ* (Philadelphia:
The Westminster Press, 1963).

pray alone is evidenced by the fact that some of His prayers have been preserved and some could not have been preserved had they not been heard.

The clearest example of Christ's group prayer is that of the ascent to the Mountain of Transfiguration, in which the overt purpose was prayer. "Now about eight days after these sayings he took with him Peter and John and James, and went up on the mountain to pray" (Luke 9:28). This is a clear answer to any who try to claim that in loyalty to Christ's teaching, we ought never to leave the closet and pray with other seeking souls. After all, He taught by example as much as by words. But even the words will not support the radical ideal of solitariness, which appears to be commanded in Matthew 6:6. Matthew also provides us with the clearest teaching about the value of sharing with others in prayer. Of what may reasonably be considered the most astonishing promise made by our Lord, Matthew gives the following account: "Again I say to you, if two of you agree on earth about anything they ask, it will be done for them by my Father in heaven" (18:19).

This striking assertion clearly refers to prayer, for it mentions petition and the Father's response. Not all of prayer is petition, but petition is central and is upheld by Christ unapologetically. The chief relevance of the astonishing promise is that it refers to prayer in which more than one is involved. The reference to two express the essence of the New Testament message. That plurality is intrinsic to the Gospel is recognized when we note that the passage about praying in one's own room is almost the only reference to individual religion to be found in the entire New Testament. Most of the New Testament is about the redemptive fellowship, and a characteristic phrase is "one another."

The only reasonable answer to the problem of aloneness and fellowship in prayer is the answer of paradox. Each individual ought to go into his closet and each individual ought to pray with the brethren, for "where two or three are gathered in my name, there am I in the midst of them" (Matt. 18:20). Fortunately, the two demands are not incompatible, because there is a time to be alone and there is also a time to be with other praying souls.

When I was a very young man I heard that great scholar, Alfred North Whitehead, give his Lowell Lectures, *Religion in the Making.* It was in these lectures that Whitehead delivered the aphorism to the effect that real religion is what a man does with his solitariness. Much as I honored the famous thinker, I knew then that he was wrong, and that he was wrong in what he tacitly excluded. Why not develop a style of life in which there are *both* solitariness and fellowship, and in which both are involved in a pattern of rhythm? We need secret prayer and we need common prayer. Francis O. Ayres has well said, "No deductions are needed to arrive at the conclusion that Christ believed in secret discipline."[8] In this the author is right, but this does not deny the complementary value of public discipline. Paradox is so intrinsic to the Gospel that we always distort the picture when we state one moment in the dialectic without the opposing or complementary moment. Jesus advised praying in secret and doing alms in secret (Matt. 6:4), but He also said, "Let your light so shine before men" (Matt. 5:16). Secrecy and witness are both valid components of the totality; they exist in unending yet beneficent tension.

The major impact of the advice about prayer is the warning against a concern for the impression we may make on the minds of other men. *We may be seen*, as Christ was seen on the mountain, but we should not pray *in order to be seen.* Here is an important warning, especially relevant to the efforts of those who are professionally religious. Once we are aware of Christ's warning, it is difficult to listen to a conventional pastoral prayer without a twinge. And how can the composers of these prayers avoid a twinge? The fashion still is that the pastor give a long prayer, carefully prepared, and that it should include, in its style, many well-rounded phrases. But why all this

[8] Francis O. Ayres, *The Ministry of the Laity* (Philadelphia: The Westminster Press, 1963), pp. 122-23.

elaborate care? The only conceivable answer is that the phrases are intended to be heard by men! The situation is made the more ironical when the man who utters the prayer is careful to use an amplifying device. It is hard not to be reminded of Christ's clearly intended humor when He says that "they have their reward." They get what they want; they are heard! The ironical pathos arises from the success of the effort. There may be a possible logical defense of the pastoral prayer, which has become standardized in Protestantism, but those whose duty it is to give such prayers should prepare themselves by frequent meditation on Matthew 6:5.

The advice which Christ gives about prayer includes the warning, "And in praying do not heap up empty phrases as the Gentiles do; for they think that they will be heard for their many words. Do not be like them, for your Father knows what you need before you ask him" (Matt. 6:7-9). It must be noted that nearly all of Christ's recorded prayers are short. The only exception is that of the so-called High Priestly prayer, to which a chapter of this book is devoted and which is clearly a special case.

Christ's counsel of brevity in vocal prayer is strongly supplemented by a parable that is wholly devoted to the practice of prayer, that of the Pharisee and the tax collector (Luke 18:9-14). It is to be noted that the prayer of the tax collector, which Christ explicitly commends, is remarkable for its humility, but is also remarkable for its brevity. The humble man beat his breast, and all that he said was "God, be merciful to me a sinner!" Sometimes, when we hear long public prayers, especially on ceremonial occasions, we wish some devout person would utter the tax collector's prayer and then sit down. It might be more effective than the conventional pattern. Or we can go further, and pray silently.

We do not need to have much experience in religious assemblies to realize how insidious is the temptation to engage in long prayers. The worst, often, are the supposedly spontaneous ones, which sometimes become collections of trite phrases. One cliché triggers another, until we are finally amazed that there is an end at all. The treasury of clichés appears to be limitless. On a recent occasion the man praying at a dinner seemed mercifully to be ending because he repeated the stock phrase "In the name of Christ," but he caught us unawares by adding "who said" and then the opportunity of going on was unlimited. It is possible to engage in public prayer without becoming enamored of the sound of one's own voice, but it is not easy. The ceremonialist is like the rich man; it is not impossible for either of them to enter the Kingdom, but it is extremely difficult.

There are many sincere followers of Christ who think that it is necessary to end every prayer with the stereotype "In the name of Christ." This is a perfect example of how we may deny the spirit of Christ's teaching on prayer by adherence to the letter. That Christ meant every prayer of His followers to end in the same way is a manifest absurdity, for this is to "heap up empty phrases." Certainly the prayer of the tax collector, which He so admired, did not end in this way. The insistence on any particular verbal form would mean a return to a pre-Christian conception of prayer.

The use of "in Christ's name" arises from overattention to certain expressions in the Fourth Gospel, such as "so that whatever you ask the Father in my name, he may give it to you" (John 15:16). Similar expressions are found in John 14:13 and in John 16:23. Nothing of this nature, however, is reported in any of the Synoptic Gospels. If the phrase is used as a necessary cliché it is absolutely indefensible, and is closer to the prayer wheel than it is to Christ. If there is anything that Christ rejects it is a required devotional formula. Professor Thomson, of Columbia Theological Seminary, is helpful at this point when he says, "To pray in Jesus' name is not simply to tack on to our prayers the formula, 'through Jesus Christ our Lord,' nor is it the equivalent to having Christ's signature to a blank check that we have filled in, and now ask the Father to honor."[9]

Emphasis on the name is completely unchristian if it is merely a linguistic device without which the prayer is not authentic, but emphasis on the name is meaningful and important if praying in Christ's name means *to pray as Christ would pray*. It means that He is our Standard, though He is also far more than that. Because praying is much more than saying prayers, we need to *learn*. The chief way in which our own feeble praying can be deepened and improved is by sustained and thoughtful acquaintance with how Christ prayed. Here is the vision of greatness which finite men require; and it must be made habitual.

The way of wisdom is to stand where the earliest followers of Christ stood and thus to ask Him to teach us to pray. Why should we not turn to Christ for a model of prayer as Keats turned to Milton for a model of verse?[10] Our prayers will naturally not be exact copies of His, for that would mean the substitution of the form for the reality. Keats's poetry was not a copy of Milton's blank verse, but nevertheless the recognition of a standard made a tremendous difference in the resultant style. Similarly, as we seek to learn from One greater than Milton, there may come to pass a real change in style in our praying. *The procedure is to soak ourselves in the model and then to pray freely.*

[9] *Op. cit.*, p. 31.
[10] See J. B. Bate, *John Keats* (Cambridge: Harvard University Press, 1964).

CHAPTER II

❦❧

Christ's Practice of Prayer

And after he had taken leave of them,
he went into the hills to pray.
Mark 6:46

W<small>HEN FIRST WE BEGIN</small> to study the Gospels, and particularly the Synoptic Gospels, we recognize some evidences of prayer on Christ's part, but we tend to think of this as a minor factor. It seems to be overshadowed by the vivid acts of healing and by the teaching, both to the multitude and to the Twelve. When we study the record more deeply, however, we begin to see that Christ's practice of prayer is evident at all points in the story. It is the foundation of all of the rest of the structure, including healing, calling, and teaching.

Sometimes we talk as though there is a conflict between the conception of continual prayer and special times devoted wholly to prayer, but Christ's practice convinces us that these two conceptions are by no means incompatible. Prayer seems to have been with him *always*, so that He could move easily from direct communication with God to direct communication with men. In this sense it is probable that His life of prayer was unbroken, always just under the surface of events. This ought to be our own standard, so that we can be engaged in prayer as we enter a room, as we face a hard decision, or as we rejoice in some undeserved good fortune, such as being prayed for or being loved. But, however much it is worth while to stress the unbroken experience, Christ's practice indicates that there is *also* a valid case to be made for times of special attention to prayer. This is surely the meaning of the fact that early in the turbulent career, He separated Himself for a while from the acts of service and made prayer the center of His attention. The output was so tremendous that there was need of inflow in order to replenish the spiritual resources. It is reasonable to apply here a sentence which appears in another context, that of the washing of the disciples' feet: "I have given you an example" (John 13:15).

One of the greatest dangers involved in the contemporary practice of prayer arises when we draw a false inference from something which is intrinsically good. It is good that our praying should be spontaneous and glad, it is good that we pray as we walk and think and speak, but it is not good to conclude from this that there is no value in specially planned times of devotion. Our prayers that are spontaneous are richer and truer if they come out of a background of disciplined regularity. The best freedom is the freedom which emerges from a life of control. That is why sincere Christians, however free they feel, soon realize that they need to establish a rule by which to live, and especially a rule by which to pray. The dean of the Episcopal Theological Seminary, of Cambridge, Massachusetts, is extremely helpful in this context:

The adoption of a rule of life is the declaration of our belief that prayer and personal religion will be developed only as we regularly and devotedly pay attention to them. It is to exercise consistently those parts of our life that have to do with our inner relation to God. This is to recognize that prayer, simply when we feel like praying or "when the spirit moves us," is never enough to build on, and that progress is never made when all is left to chance or our emotions. A rule of life affirms that, once having decided what is everlastingly true concerning our devotional life, we then commit ourselves to the best way we know of getting there and abide by the rule as well as we can, come what may.[1]

[1] John B. Coburn, *Prayer and Personal Religion* (Philadelphia: The Westminster Press, 1957), p. 77.

Even the great William Law, the strongest of all exponents of the idea that "devotion is neither private nor public prayer, but a life given to God" and that "a good Christian should consider every place as holy," upholds the idea that special times are needed, chiefly because men and women are weak and forgetful. He says, "This much, I believe, is certain: the generality of Christians ought to use forms of prayer at all the regular times of prayer."[2] Later, he says, when a man's heart is ready, "he should leave his form for a while."

It is a little shocking to realize that Christ, on occasion, actually neglected the needy populace for a while in order to pray. The striking instance of this phenomenon is that of going apart from the clamoring crowd to the Mountain of Transfiguration. All three of the Synoptics tell the story, but only Luke, who stresses prayer more than do the others, says that He went up to *pray* (9:28). Most of the disciples remained on the plain below, continuing to meet with, and trying to help, the needy people. Yet Christ Himself, with His inner circle, actually seemed to avoid, at least for a time, the human miseries which He could have relieved had He been there. We know of the miseries because the needy people were there waiting for Him upon His return.

Here is the finest example of the rhythm of withdrawal and encounter. It would have been a mistake to *remain* always on the mountain, but it would also have been a mistake never to *ascend* the mountain. Service is important, but service is not the only thing that is important. In so far as we try to imitate the life of Christ, we need to be reminded that the quality of service depends primarily upon what we have to *offer*, and that we do not have enough to offer when we are always offering. Christ left the needy people in order to engage in prayer, not because He did not care, but because He cared so much that He had to have times apart for conscious communion with the Father. The duty to pray is as crucial as is the duty to serve.

[2] William Law, *A Serious Call to a Devout and Holy Life* (Philadelphia: The Westminster Press, 1955), pp. 17, 31, 91.

Though the prayer on the Mountain of Transfiguration was with a little company, several of the recorded times of spiritual renewal were spent in solitude. Matthew informs us that the shock of the news of John's martyrdom, as one result of the debauchery of the corrupt Herodian court, drove Christ into solitude. "Now when Jesus heard this, he withdrew from there in a boat to a lonely place apart" (14:13). It is easy to see that the death of John came as a very great blow. After all, it was through the instrumentality of John's witness that at the Jordan, His vision of His own work in the world had begun to come clear. The beheading of John also brought to full attention the apparent success of unprincipled power. Only in solitude could this combination be faced.

Sometimes Christ separated the Apostles from the strain of human encounter by taking them apart with Him, when their need was sufficient. "And he said to them, 'Come away by yourselves to a lonely place, and rest a while'" (Mark 6:31). Here is the support for the requirement that busy people, especially those in the serving, healing, and teaching occupations, should engage in periodic retreats. These withdrawals do not involve failure, or any backward motion, but rather a gathering of resources for renewed encounter. They are really advances rather than retreats. Every busy life should be lived in chapters, including chapters devoted to work and chapters devoted to preparation for work. With the world-wide increase in population, the experience of absolute solitude is becoming daily more difficult, but for most of us it is still possible, providing it is included in a conscious and deliberate plan. Most people in public life would accomplish far more if each could have one week in the year when he does not see even one other human being. The relief from having to impress, or even to please, is potentially healing.

It is in Luke's account that we have the most dramatic evidence of the outpouring of energy with the consequent need of withdrawal:

Now when the sun was setting, all those who had any that were sick with various diseases brought them to him; and he laid his hands on every one of them and healed them. And demons also came out of many, crying, "You are the Son of God!" But he rebuked them, and would not allow them to speak, because they knew that he was the Christ. And when it was day he departed and went into a lonely place. [4:40-42]

A great part of the dramatic effect of this scene is involved in the fact that Christ's solitude could not be maintained for very long. The pathetic conclusion of the scene is "And the people sought him and came to him, and would have kept him from leaving them."

A similar instance of withdrawal is that which comes after Jesus has asked, without success, that His healing of a leper should not be spread abroad: "But so much the more the report went abroad concerning him; and great multitudes gathered to hear and to be healed of their infirmities. But he withdrew to the wilderness and prayed" (Luke 5:15-16). Again we read: "And after He had dismissed the crowds, he went up into the hills by himself to pray" (Matt. 14:23).

Professor Thomson has counted seventeen different references in the four Gospels to Christ's practice of prayer, and if, to these, we add the implied references, they are numerous indeed.[3] The praying emerges on all kinds of occasions, including those of joy as well as those of manifest strain. When Christ prayed in connection with food, He was following the Jewish practice. Examples of this are found in Mark 6:41, John 6:11, and especially in the following: "And commanding the crowd to sit down on the ground, he took the seven loaves and the fish, and *having given thanks* he broke them and gave them to the disciples, and the disciples gave them to the crowd's (Matt. 15:35-36). All three Synoptic authors report prayer in connection with the Last Supper or Paschal feast, while the Apostle Paul also included this feature in his own

[3] *The Praying Christ, op. cit.,* p. 35.

account of the famous meal (I Cor. 11:24). Luke's statement is "And he took bread, and when he had given thanks he broke it" (22:19). Matthew and Mark also refer to a prayer of thanks over the cup. Even after the resurrection, thankful prayer accompanied the sharing of food on the road to Emmaus: "When he was at table with them, he took the bread and blessed" (Luke 24:30). Clearly, prayer appears from the beginning to the end.

Prayer seems to have accompanied particular acts of healing, as illustrated in the healing of the man who was deaf and had an impediment in his speech. With an impressive courtesy, Christ took the man aside so as not to make his healing into a spectacle. The man, who was obviously suffering from extreme nervousness, as the impediment in speech indicated, certainly needed to be free from the stares of the surrounding crowd. Therefore he was healed *privately!* The story is unique to Mark's Gospel and we are grateful for it because it enables us to speak accurately of the courtesy of Jesus. But to the courtesy was added prayer, even though the report of it is fragmentary. "And looking up to heaven, he sighed" (Mark 7:34).

When our Lord came down from the Mountain of Transfiguration, where He had prayed, He found that the followers who had remained on the plain with the needy crowd were unsuccessful in their effort to heal a boy who was convulsed and foaming at the mouth. After the boy was healed in Christ's presence, the disciples asked Him privately the reason for their own failure. Then came the trenchant answer, "This kind cannot be driven out by anything but prayer" (Mark 9:29). The inference is that the unsuccessful followers of Christ had engaged in exorcism without prayer. The boy was healed, then, when Christ really prayed for him and not before. The raising of Lazarus likewise shows the association of prayer with deeds of compassion. Before the raising of this man who had been dead four days, "Jesus lifted up his eyes and said, 'Father, I thank thee that thou hast heard me. I know that thous hearest me always' " (John 11:41-42).

One reference to Christ at prayer concerns a prayer for one individual, Peter, though there is no reason to suppose that such prayerful solicitude was unique. That the man with the humorous nickname, so obviously at variance with his real character, was deeply in need of prayer, was clear. Even with the prayer, Peter failed for a time and was overtly disloyal, though later he demonstrated a firmness which Christ apparently recognized as potential all along. To Simon, Christ said, "I have prayed for you that your faith may not fail; and when you have turned again, strengthen your brethren" (Luke 22:32). The first part of the prayer was temporarily not answered, but the latter part was eventually answered with tremendous effectiveness. The man who resembled worthless rubble eventually did resemble a rock.

The most striking examples of Christ's praying are those associated with the major crises of His public life. Each big decision had to be faced with prayer because nothing else was adequate. The first of these crises was that of the baptism, which introduced the entire public career. So far as we know, this was the first major opening in Christ's life. For the other people who gathered with John at the Jordan, the probability is that all that occurred was a ceremonial occasion. There is no reason to suppose that the others who were present heard the heavenly voice, but the important fact is that Christ heard it. We do not really know what it means for the Spirit to descend "like a dove" except that the figure indicates quietness and modesty of effect. It did not come as a roaring lion or as a screaming eagle. The voice was for Christ alone; it addressed itself to the second person singular. "Thou art my beloved Son; with thee I am well pleased" (Luke 3:22). We owe to Luke the valuable information that the experience of being called to a great and divine vocation came while Jesus was praying. "And when Jesus also had been baptized and *was praying*, the heaven was opened (3:21).

There is no way in which we can exaggerate the crucial

importance of the baptismal experience. It is not that the water was important or that the ceremony had any magical significance. Indeed, John himself had already minimized this aspect of the experience by saying, "I baptize you with water; but he who is mightier than I is coming. . . . he will baptize you with the Holy Spirit and with fire" (Luke 3:16). The same theme is picked up later, when real baptism is mentioned as something in the future, and the figure of fire, suggested by John, is taken seriously: "I came to cast fire upon the earth; and would that it were already kindled! I have a baptism to be baptized with; and how I am constrained until it is accomplished!" (Luke 12:49-50). The risen Christ was still referring to John, including the fact of the incompleteness of John's message: "John baptized with water, but before many days you shall be baptized with the Holy Spirit" (Acts 1:5).

The impact of John's vitality must have been immense in so far as the mind of Christ was concerned. John was the instrument of arousing. There is no reason to suppose that the prayer at the baptism was the first instance of prayer in the experience of our Lord, but we do know that it is the first *recorded* instance. The crisis was so great that prayer was the only appropriate response.

There is a moving reminder of the consciousness of the debt to John in the fact that Christ, in one of his frequent withdrawals from the hubbub, went back to the scene of the first revolutionary experience. "He went away again across the Jordan to the place where John at first baptized, and there he remained" (John 10:40). Such a sentimental journey is not hard to understand. It is reasonable to have a close attachment to particular places, especially places in which crucial events have occurred. Doctor Samuel Johnson definitively expressed the meaning of such attachment in his account of one stop on his tour of the Hebrides, viz., the stop at the fabulous island of Iona. "Far from me and from my friends," he wrote, "be such frigid philosophy as may conduct us indifferent and unmoved over any ground which has been dignified by wisdom, bravery or virtue. That man is little to be envied, whose patriotism would not gain force upon the plain of Marathon, or whose piety would not grow warmer among the ruins of Iona." The New Testament gives not one mention of a Christian shrine, but it does record the deliberate attempt, on Christ's part, to enjoy a visible reminder of a really decisive occasion. For our present purposes the occasion is memorable because of prayer at the time.

New Testament scholars have learned, through the method of form criticism, to be aware of the possibility of a sharp contrast between the particular literary form, such as an individual parable, and the historical narrative which cements the various units together. The common speculation is that the historical connections have been added with some freedom on the part of editorial writers. It is for this reason that emphasis on significance of sequence is often suspect. It is to be noted, however, that this criticism does not apply in the instance of the baptism because the praying is intrinsic to the event. It was *while* He was praying that the opening occurred.

Form criticism has taught us to be on the alert for passages reflecting the Church's later experience in preaching or liturgy or catechetical instruction which were read back into the narrative of Christ's life by the authors. It is possible for this to have happened because all of the Gospels were written after some of the public experiences of early Christians had begun to develop a pattern. This cannot reasonably apply to the baptism story, however, because the baptism administered by John could hardly be confused with Christian baptism. After all, John was not a Christian, and Christ, in Luke 12:50, speaks of *His* baptism as in the future.

The second major crisis in Christ's public life was that of the choosing of the Twelve. The very idea of the Twelve was one of transcendent importance. There was nothing unique about having disciples, or students, or followers. Socrates had disciples and so had John the Baptist. There were even disciples of the Pharisees, as we learn in Mark 2:18. The new thing was to have *Apostles*, a group of ordinary men trained to be a task force and prepared to carry on when the Master's earthly life should be ended. The exact number of the Twelve may have been adopted as reminiscent of the twelve tribes of Israel, but it is clear that the whole conception is pointed forward, and is not primarily concerned with anything anti-quarian. The Twelve represented the best hope of securing continuing vitality and actually became the link between Christ and the ongoing Church, which, with all its failures, has a record of amazing success both in sheer endurance and in effectiveness in the world. The gates of hell have not been able to prevail against it!

The work of Christ is sharply contrasted with that of John the Baptist, in a strategic sense, in that Christ developed an apostolic band while John did not. Consequently, John's was a voice crying in the wilderness without continuing impact. It is no exaggeration to say that Christ's decision to select the Twelve was one of the crucial decisions of the world. There is no reason to suppose that we should ever have heard of the gospel apart from this carefully conceived step. Without this step the teaching of Christ might easily have been one of the bubbles which eventually burst and which were mentioned by Gamaliel in Acts 5:36-37. Our Lord was a Teacher, but it was not His work as a Teacher that made endurance pos-sible; it was His work as the creator of a small redemptive society. Only through such a society could the gospel become salt to keep the world from decay and leaven to make the dough rise. Since Christ wrote no book, He depended entirely upon the faithfulness of the prepared group. Not all of them understood Him or proved faithful, yet, in the end, the method succeeded. The present existence of the Church is the evi-dence that the method was fundamentally sound.

There is every reason to suppose that Christ took very seri-ously the selection of the members of the redemptive task force. In the long run it was obvious that the quality of the members would make or break the new movement. And, because human freedom of decision is a fact, there was no way of having absolute insurance about the outcome. The decision was to select from among the many disciples a few who exhibited the greatest promise and then to concentrate on them.

The sending out of the Twelve represents a genuine turning point, and one which, according to Mark, came immediately after the failure at Nazareth. The Temple had emphasized ceremonial, and had little to do with any regular congregation; the synagogue was devoted chiefly to instruction, with incidental prayers added; the new movement was centered in what we can only call a missionary band. Their characteristic direction of movement was "out," and when they gathered they did so only as a preparation for scattering. Mark 6:7, therefore, signifies a genuine watershed.

It is not very surprising, in the light of the crucial nature of the decision about selection, that Christ faced this particular experience with prayer. In a deep sense, this was the real beginning of the Church, for the Church does not consist of individual listeners. The Church, when it is genuine, consists in the transformation of disciples into apostles. Again, as in the account of the baptism, the praying cannot be separated from the decision, as form criticism might seem to indicate, because the prayer is intrinsic to the event. Mark states it very simply as follows: "And he went up into the hills, and called to him those whom he desired" (3:13). The isolation from the world and the selection are thus two parts of one event. Luke is even more specific, stressing the time element. "In these days he went out into the hills to pray; and all night he continued in prayer to God. And when it was day, he called his disciples, and chose from them twelve, whom he named apostles" (6:12-13). It is difficult to see how any Christian can read these words without deep emotion. They tell a magnificent story with amazing compactness and restraint.

Many have noted the reference to the whole night in prayer, but it cannot be mentioned too often. The account gives us one of the best insights into what Christ's practice of prayer really was. Here we are far from mere ceremonial, as we are also far from any insistence upon spoken form. The decision was so crucial that it had to be faced in long hours of effort in order to know what the Father's will might be. Few accounts can make us so unsatisfied with our own feeble, hurried, or purely verbal prayers as does this one. Alcibiades was reported, in *The Symposium*, as saying that Socrates was the only person who ever made him feel shame. In a far greater fashion, most of us can say that Christ's whole night of prayer, in selecting the Twelve, makes us bitterly ashamed of our conventional and hurried praying.

The chief insight we may gain from Christ's experience in choosing the Twelve is that regarding what we call today the existential situation. Prayer grows in depth and power when there is a mood of urgency, and urgency comes with consciousness of decision. Real choice is always agonizing to a thoughtful individual, because he is bound to see that some choices eliminate others. He will think often of "the road not taken." What would my life be now if I had made a different decision at any one of many points? The truth is that I could have chosen otherwise, for it is part of the uniqueness of man that he is partially indeterminate. Christ could have avoided the choosing of the Twelve; He *could* have chosen others than the ones whose names we know. How different the world might be in consequence! For one thing, it is highly doubtful if, in that case, we should use our present system of dating. The philosophy of existentialism would be better understood if people were to meditate more on the choosing of the Twelve.

The third obvious crisis in Christ's public career involved the understanding, on the part of the Twelve, of who He was. It is a little shocking to realize that they followed Him *before* they recognized Him as the expected Messiah, but such is the case. All of the Synoptic Gospels record the sudden recognition by Simon as coming fairly late in the story, and this is not really surprising when we contemplate the vast difference between the way in which He appeared and the forms which the appearance of the Messiah were popularly expected to take. Even Peter, advanced as his insight was, immediately rejected the idea of a suffering Messiah, and had to be silenced (Matt. 16:22-23).

The selection of the membership of the Twelve was important, as has already been indicated, but, if they were to perform their redemptive function, they needed to understand the cosmic significance of their undertaking. Therefore, out of Christ's experience of prayer came the question that triggered their insight. We owe to Luke the realization that the praying and the question were part of one incident. This helps us to understand how, if we seek, however unworthily, to imitate Christ in prayer, we should expect the prayer to eventuate in vivid intellectual activity. The relevant passage, as Luke records it, is "One day when he was praying alone in the presence of his disciples, he asked them, 'Who do the people say I am?'" (9:18, NEB). The apparent inconsistency about praying alone, yet with disciples, is solved if we suppose that His prayer was silent and therefore unhindered by the fact that others were present.

What we learn from this justaposition is that prayer need not be separated from thinking or from action. Temporarily, the little band was separate *from* the world, but what transpired was *for* the world. Thought and prayer need not be separated, but can stimulate each other if we try to follow the pattern which Christ has given. One consequence is that the experience of worship, even of public worship, need not be a time of intellectual vacuity. Indeed, there are many who can testify to the fact that prayer, either alone or with the fellowship, is often the occasion for the most intense intellectual activity. Sometimes, in the white heat of prayer, ideas fuse to form new unities, when they cannot fuse in colder environments. That prayer may lead to insight should not be in the least surprising; it is not so rare as is ordinarily supposed.

The fourth great crisis was that of the crucifixion. As former crises have led us to expect, this final crisis was associated with prayer, both preceding and during the crucifixion. The situation is different, however, since in the final crisis we have fragmentary records of the actual prayers, whereas in the first three crises we have only references to the fact that Christ was praying. We can, therefore, deal with the prayers in the Garden of Gethsemane and on the cross in separate chapters, and need not discuss them in the present chapter. Suffice it to say now that they complete the pattern of recourse to prayer as the natural step in high and agonizing moments.

The connection between crisis prayers and prayer all of the time is important to keep in mind, for while there is contrast between them, there is no conflict. Christ's praying was *habitual*, but it could also be *special*. George Buttrick states the point with his usual succinctness when he says, in one of his Harvard sermons, that Christ lived "instant in crisis-prayer, constant in prayer's vigil."[4] We have known a few persons in our time who can move effortlessly into vocal prayer in any discussion, and, though they tend to make us a bit uncomfortable, we must admit that they are closer to Christ's own practice than is the case with those of us who pride ourselves on more self-conscious restraint.

Two of the parables, both of which are unique to Luke, bear directly on the constant or persistent aspect of prayer, and were undoubtedly told with the purpose of clarifying this point. These are the parables of the Importunate Friend and of the Unjust Judge. The first of these which Luke, with the obvious intention of connecting it with prayer, places immediately after the Pattern Prayer (see below, p. 45), is the story of a man who has the uncomfortable experience of having an unexpected and hungry friend arriving at midnight. Since the householder has no food prepared, he goes in desperation to the house of a neighbor to ask for the loan of three loaves. The neighbor is naturally unwilling to be disturbed in the middle of the night, saying, "Do not bother

[4] *Sermons Preached in a University Church, op. cit.,* p. 17.

me; the door is now shut, and my children are with me in bed; I cannot get up and give you anything" (11:7).

We can sympathize with the neighbor who has gone to bed, but the point of the story is that he does finally get up and loan the loaves, not because he is friendly, but because the man making the request is so insistent. Finally it is easier to grant the request than to keep on being pestered.

When we name this the Parable of Successful Pestering, we see how it is possible for Christ to combine real humor with an important truth. That the parable was intended to be humorous is highly probable, and it is easy to see that the first listeners must have laughed. That may be why they remembered a story so mundane. Most of us sometimes accede to requests, for money or for service or even invitations to share in hospitality, simply because it is less troublesome to acquiesce than it is to go on saying "No."

Light as the parable apparently is, it involves a profound truth. When applied to prayer, it means that success comes by unlimited persistence. Why should we not be as importunate in our effort to achieve communion with the Father as the householder was on a relatively trivial occasion? Why not put the same persistence into big enterprises which we employ in little things?

The other parable of persistence, that of the Unjust Judge (Luke 18:1-5), makes the same point, though it is not humorous as that of the midnight request is. Both refer to successful pestering, but the second differs from the earlier in that Luke specifically connects the story with the need of unending prayer. "And he told them a parable, to the effect that they ought always to pray and not lose heart" (18:1). The obvious point is that if persistence pays off, even with unjust persons, how much more reasonable must it be to employ it in connection with the loving Father.

George Buttrick helps us, partly by his frank acceptance of the fact that the two parables of prayer "are in some respects difficult to construe." "We can be sure," he writes, "that Jesus does not mean us to regard God as either a callous judge or a grudging neighbor, for such a translation would flatly contradict all else taught by the Gospels. Some items in the story are only for verisimilitude. But the requirement of persistence in prayer is unmistakable."[5] There is no reason to make every item meaningful. Certainly the sleepy householder does not represent God, because he does the right thing for the wrong reason. God must not be represented as one who needs to be cajoled, and prayer must not be presented as a device by which we wring from a grudging Father what He does not want to give us. Prayer is not an overcoming of God's reluctance, for He already wants the best for us. It is not because God's will needs to be changed, but because of our own weakness and ineptitude that prayer must be continuous and persistent.

When Professor John Baillie, of New York and Edinburgh, died, he left a number of sermons which have since been published. Perhaps the finest of them is his sermon on the parable which we may term that of the Importunate Widow, rather than that of the Unjust Judge, as is conventionally done. The parable, Baillie said,

represents our Lord's teaching about prayer in what many would regard as its extremest form. Nowhere in the religious literature of the world can we find stronger statements about the power and efficacy of prayer than we find in the preaching of Jesus, and this parable of the importunate widow has often been felt to be the strongest statement of all. Jesus is here telling us what we are to do when we have prayed and prayed again and our prayer has apparently not made the slightest difference to anything. And what He does is not offer us any alternative method of obtaining our desire, but simply to say, "Go on praying all the harder, all the more importunately."[6]

The point which this simple parable makes so effectively is essentially the same as that which Christ makes in His com-

---

[5] Buttrick, *Prayer* (Nashville: Abingdon Press, 1942), p. 33.
[6] Baillie, *Christian Devotion* (New York: Charles Scribner's Sons, 1962), p. 43.

mand to ask and to go on asking. The major statement of this, which is practically identical in Matthew and in Luke, and probably was drawn by both of them from an original collection of sayings, is as follows: "Ask, and it will be given you; seek, and you will find; knock, and it will be opened to you. For every one who asks receives, and he who seeks finds, and to him who knocks it will be opened" (Matt. 7:7-8). Because God loves us truly, far more than any human father can love his children, we can be sure, says Jesus, that the Father who is in heaven will "give good things to those who ask Him." The lesson is that the asking must never stop.

A subtle aspect of the Parable of the Importunate Friend is the way in which the persistent request is really intercessory. The man who pestered his neighbor was concerned with the need of another, rather than any need of his own. As we grow in the practice of prayer, and as we follow more closely the example of Christ, our prayers become more largely intercessory. Though Christ did not hesitate to pray for Himself, He prayed more for others. In the light of Christ's experience, there is no adequate reason for not engaging in intercessory prayer for anybody about whom we care, or even about those who hate us. What clearer case of the command for intercession is there than the injunction to pray for our enemies (Matt. 5:44 and Luke 6:28)?

Many in our generation have expressed strong misgivings about the kind of prayer which, to be effective, necessarily seems to contravene the process of natural law. This misgiving is especially great when germs are involved or when we face natural calamities such as earthquake, flood, or drought. It is not hard to envisage Christ's answer to this problem. Of course there are natural laws, and germs are real existents, but these are not ultimate. They are secondary, and only God's loving purpose is primary. Therefore, we need not be finicky about what we ask in prayer. If we ask for the wrong things perhaps the event will teach us, but the decision concerning what is a valid request in prayer, and what is not, is not ours to make.

If this is God's world and if we are His children, made in His image, it is reasonable to open our hearts in prayer as a child opens his heart to his parent. The good parent does not desire that the child shall be self-consciously anxious about which requests are valid and which are not. What is desirable is the unobstructed communion of spirits. So is it with us in regard to the Father, Jesus teaches us both by precept and by example. Much of prayer ought to consist of elements other than petition, such as thanksgiving and praise, but this does not mean that petition is inappropriate. Christ asked! Why should not we who seek to be His humble followers do the same?

CHAPTER III

❦ ❧

The Pattern Prayer

> "This is how you should pray."
> *Matthew* 6:9 (NEB)

THE BEST-KNOWN PRAYER of our Lord is almost universally misnamed. It is called the Lord's Prayer when it is clearly a prayer designed for the use of His *followers*. If we did not know this in any other way, we should know it because of the fact that it includes a request for forgiveness of sin. If Christ needed to ask for forgiveness, we have been entirely mistaken in our general judgment about Him. The prayer in question, which millions know by heart, is a very great prayer, but it is actually the *Disciples' Prayer*. The words were suggested by Christ, but it is not His in the sense that He is known to have prayed it. In this regard the prayer is in sharp contrast to others which are examined in succeeding chapters of this book.

The "Our Father" differs from all other prayers suggested or employed by Christ in that it very early became an established unit in Christian worship and remains so to this day. In the world-wide Anglican communion the "Our Father" is employed in both Morning and Evening Prayer, and is used twice in the celebration of Holy Communion. It is also used in Confirmation, Matrimony, and the Burial of the Dead. There is probably no single form of words which Christians

45

have repeated more often when they have assembled together for worship.

The wide public use of this prayer is easily understandable, even though that use involves some degree of anomaly. The New Testament includes various phrases which scholars believe to be parts of early Christian worship, each of which was read back into the beginnings, apparently under the apprehension that they were actually primitive expressions. There is no evidence that Christ gave any directions about the conduct of worship, and, furthermore, the entire New Testament contains not a single order of worship. Slight suggestions of what went on when Christians gathered are found in I Corinthians 14:26-33 and in Colossians 3:16, and there is a little said about the Lord's Supper in I Corinthians 11:23-29, but that is about all.

There is every reason to believe that the gatherings of early Christians were highly informal, that there were many vocal participants, as Paul indicates, and that no sharp separation was made between worship and strategic planning. The members of the primitive Church met, primarily, not to go through a ceremony, something which they did not have and probably did not desire to have, but "to teach and admonish one another in all widsom" (Col. 3:16). It was natural that they should add "psalms and hymns and spiritual songs," because the people were thankful in their hearts and had much to sing about. But there is no evidence at all of an established liturgy in the earliest Church, and certainly no hard-and-fast distinction, such as came later, between clergy and laity.

When the early enthusiasm was somewhat lessened, and the primitive fire had begun to die down, there was a natural tendency to formalize practices, especially the practices of public worship. What should it include? Naturally, it would include prayer, and what we normally call the Lord's Prayer seemed to be a godsend for this purpose, because it was given by Christ Himself and thus had the ring of authenticity. It seemed to be the next best thing to an officially prescribed liturgy. And even though they have been almost certainly mistaken in the judgment, it has undoubtedly been the judgment of many that the "Our Father" *is* an officially prescribed liturgical formula.

Hallowed as the prayer is by long and almost universal use, there is no good reason to suppose that Christ intended to provide His followers with a formal prayer for rote memorization and ceremonial usage. According to both Matthew and Luke, the prayer emerged, not from any discussion of liturgy, but as a climax to instruction about how the individual should pray. Luke says that Christ was praying in a certain place and that when He had finished, one of His followers asked Him to teach him and others how to pray. This request must have arisen both from a sense of need and from admiration for the obvious reality of Christ's praying. Luke says (11:3-4) that Christ answered the man by listing five basic requests as follows:

> For reverence
> For the Kingdom
> For daily bread
> For forgiveness
> For help in testing times.

Though Matthew's version[1] is not identical with Luke's, it involves the same five requests, the chief difference being their slight elaboration.[2] On the whole it is Matthew's version that has normally been used as an expression of public prayer. In the *Book of Common Prayer* there is always added, following certain early manuscripts of Matthew's text, "For thine is the kingdom, and the power, and the glory, for ever and ever. Amen."[3] The Authorized English Version of 1611 included

---

[1] A third version is found in the *Didache*, but it is virtually identical with that in Matthew. See *Didache* 8:2.

[2] Because of Matthew's apparent elaboration it is usually held that Luke's shorter version is closer to the original. For example, he begins with the simple salutation, "Father."

[3] In Hebrew practice it was not uncommon to add a doxology even though it was not in the printed text. For a similar doxology see I Chron. 29:11:

this doxology, but it has been omitted from most contemporary translations, including the Revised Standard Version and *The New English Bible*. The general judgment of scholars is that this passage reflects later liturgical usage and is not in the mood of the prayer itself. The fact that we now have the use of manuscripts earlier than any known to the translators appointed by King James in the early seventeenth century is an important advantage.

According to Matthew, the Pattern Prayer emerged from a session devoted to instruction in the practice of prayer, the instruction continuing after the pattern was given by the added emphasis on one particular request. The process is exceedingly simple: Christ tells His followers something in general about prayer, including certain dangers, and then He provides a concrete illustration of what He is saying. The pattern is introduced by the words, "Pray then like this" (6:9). The strongest reason for supposing that He was not providing a stereotype, to be memorized and used on all occasions, is that He had just warned His followers, when they prayed, not to "heap up empty phrases as the Gentiles do" (6:7). It is easy to see what He had in mind. The formation of official prayers to be rattled off, frequently with no concern for their meaning, is one of the most common features in the history of religious practices, some of which are included in "Gentile" religions. Unless we are very careful, this is what will happen to the finest and best. Some boast that they can race through their prescribed devotion in record time. The prayer wheel can be turned faster and faster!

This is the really terrible thing that has happened to the Lord's Prayer. How sad that Christ's very attempt to help men to escape from meaningless rote should sometimes *become* meaningless rote. Yet we must admit, in all honesty, that this is what it is for many today. We are so familiar with

---

"Thine, O Lord, is the greatness, and the power, and the glory, and the victory, and the majesty; for all that is in the heavens and in the earth is thine; thine is the kingdom, O Lord, and thou art exalted as head above all."

the words of the "Our Father" that we can repeat them with no effort at all, and sometimes with no serious recognition of what we are saying. There is, in this, an element of ultimate blasphemy. One of the chief ways to deny Christ is to turn any of His words into what He called "empty phrases."

Since we are not likely to be able to reverse the practice of using liturgically what was not intended for that purpose at all, we can at least concentrate upon the task of trying to recover, in so far as is possible, the meaning of the words which we repeat. In this we are helped by meditating on the revolutionary nature of Christ's approach to faith. He seems to have had no interest in that kind of worship which tends to be limited to sacred places, and the ceremonies of the Temple were not His concern. Not only did He say, "Something greater than the temple is here" (Matt. 12:6); He ignored almost wholly the throngs of priests who served in the Temple. And to the woman at the well of Samaria, who asked *which* sacred place was the one, He answered, as He often did, by indicating that she had asked the wrong question. "Believe me," He said, "the time is coming when you will worship the Father neither on this mountain, nor in Jerusalem" (John 4:21, NEB). Worship, He indicated, is something bigger than place or than prescribed liturgical form. Our terrible mistake is to make small what is meant to be large.

In stressing the five objects of prayer, as mentioned in Christ's pattern, we are evidently getting close to what was original. The essential agreement of Matthew and Luke, in spite of linguistic differences, is impressive, and the directness is what we are led to expect from a similar directness in other parts of Christ's teaching. It is not necessary to claim that all of the items were original with Christ. In fact, several of them are similar in tone to various Hebrew prayers, and "Our Father who art in heaven" does not seem at all strange to anyone familiar with the Hebrew Prayer Book of our own day, in which God is addressed as "King of the Universe." What Christ did was not to invent absolutely new forms, but rather to emphasize the important by inspired selection. The most remarkable feature of the "Our Father" is not what it includes, but what it omits. It is prayer reduced to essentials.[4]

The first of the five items is notable for its emphasis upon God rather than upon ourselves and our need. In one sense the love of God and the love of fellow men are equal, but, in another sense, the love of God deserves priority. Reverence is the note on which to begin, Christ seems to say. Much of our danger lies in failure to remember who we are, and in a consequent arrogance. The only way in which we can see ourselves aright is in the context of the being and glory of God, whose humble servants we may eventually become. However hard we work, we recognize, when we are honest, that we are not self-made creatures, and that what is best in our lives comes by grace rather than by our own deserts.

The beginning of prayer, then, is the recognition that God really *is*, that the more knowledge a man has, the more humble he feels and the more aware he is of his own ignorance. The finest scientist is often the man who is aware that his greatest observations are discoveries rather than inventions and that, at best, he is thinking God's thoughts after Him. The most unlovely of human poses is that of self-conceit, and the surest antidote to this pose is humble reverence. This is precisely what is involved in the phrase "Hallowed be thy Name."

It is hard for us in the modern world to understand or to appreciate the Hebrew's sense of mystery about a name, and particularly about the name of God. The name of God stood for God's character, for God's integrity, and for God's active power. We are familiar with references to the name in the Psalms, particularly "He leadeth me in the paths of righteousness for his name's sake" (23:3, AV) and "Save me, O God, by thy name" (54:1). To call on God's name meant to involve His power and to claim His promises. Perhaps we can under-

---

[4] Cf. Buttrick, *Prayer, op. cit.*, p. 29: "The uniqueness of the teaching of Jesus is its wholeness, its proportion—that is, in what it made central or circumferential."

stand this better if we remind ourselves of the sacredness of the *signature* in our culture. Many a man honors his signature, even at great personal cost, yet it is only a written name. If we thus dignify a name, even today, is it so surprising that names often had almost mystical significance in ancient times? The name of God is only the extreme instance. G. W. Anderson, professor of Old Testament Studies at the University of Durham, says, accordingly, that "the name aptly expresses the continued manifestation of the divine nature in Yahweh's dealings with his people."[5]

The Hebrew people placed strong emphasis on the confrontation between Moses and the Living God as recorded in Exodus 3:13-14. Moses asked God's name and was told that the name is a form of the verb "to be." "And God said unto Moses, *I am that I am*" (AV). Yahweh, then, is "He who is." Here the tremendous emphasis is on the real being of God, in contrast with illusion or with mere projections of desire. God, according to this conception, is not remote or the object of speculation, but is the real Being of continued self-manifestation. The paradox here is that the emphasis on the name is the exact antithesis of what we call nominalism.

The second basic request advised by Christ goes beyond reverence to action. We are told to pray for the Kingdom, which is defined as that situation in which God's will is made manifest on earth. Our prayer is that that which is potential may become actual, here and now. We are keenly aware of how far from such a situation we, in fact, are. God's will is not now perfectly done, perhaps not anywhere. If it *were* already done, there would be no point in praying for it! God's will is not done because He has created men for freedom, and part of our freedom is involved in the fact that God does not coerce His children; He lets them oppose Him! There is a deep sense in which God's will, we believe, must eventually be supreme, but now it is not supreme, because it is not

[5] *Peake's Commentary* (London and New York: Thomas Nelson and Sons, Ltd., 1962), p. 162.

supreme in us. The Kingdom is not actualized so long as there are any who actively oppose the Father's will.

Christ makes the idea of the Kingdom wonderfully clear in the Pattern Prayer by uniting it with God's will. Thus it becomes intensely practical. Each of us can pray "Thy will be done, beginning with me." The ultimate sin is self-centeredness, i.e., substituting our wills for what we know of the divine will. We mistake the Kingdom request greatly if we think that *we* are the chief actors in the drama. We may be needed, but the fundamental work for which we pray is God's work. Professor K. Stendahl, of Harvard, says that the Pattern Prayer, in its second petition, "asks for the establishment of the Kingdom of God, by God for us, not by us for God."[6]

The tragedy is that, though we are made for freedom, we are not really free, for we are bound by our own self-centeredness. We put ourselves where we ought to put God. Thus Christ teaches, in his doctrine of freedom, that real freedom is not something with which we start. It comes at the end of a process, rather than at the beginning, and it comes only by definite steps, of which He mentions four. "If you continue in my word, you are truly my disciples, and you will know the truth, and the truth will make you free" (John 8:31-32). It is a shame that the full, fourfold proposition is seldom remembered when the latter part is separated from its context and used as an inscription on public buildings. In any case, it is important for us to know that the doing of God's will, as free agents, is a costly process. Whether the Kingdom will finally come all at once is beyond our knowledge, and Christ specifically warns against the untrustworthiness of forecasters (Mark 13:2 and Matt. 24:23), but in any event we know that our present task is that of bringing as much as we can of the present world into conformity with God's will, as revealed by Christ. This is why it is not unreasonable to speak of the Kingdom of Christ.

[6] *Ibid.*, p. 778.

In the pattern of petition suggested by Christ the third request is for something exceedingly mundane: daily bread. There are always people about us who think that they are called upon to be merely spiritual and who therefore are critical of any who ask for things. Whatever ground they stand on, in this regard, they cannot claim the authority of Christ. Bread is intensely material and Christ advises that we ask for it, not in some metaphorical sense, but as something required for daily sustenance. Because the prayer is closely related to daily life, the tense is important and seems to suggest tomorrow as well as today, though scholars are divided because of the obscurity of the Greek word involved.[7] In any case, we shall not live unless we continue to eat, and bread clearly stands for the food that is required.

It is not unreasonable to make bread refer, by extension, to all of our material needs, including clothing and shelter.[8] We are not disembodied spirits and we do not desire to be. We owe to several thinkers, but especially to the great Archbishop William Temple, the exciting idea that Christianity is not merely or primarily a spiritual religion. Christianity, Temple pointed out more than once, is the most material of all the world's religions. Whenever men are truly followers of Christ, they build hospitals for broken and sick bodies; they feed the hungry; and they distribute clothing. The soul is of central importance, but so long as we are in the flesh, we must be treated as whole persons. To say that what happens to our bodies is unimportant is simply not true. Therefore, our spiritual message is not likely to mean much to hungry people unless we first help them to be fed. The philosophy of Christ is the philosophy of wholeness.

It is hard for members of an affluent society to realize how

[7] The word which we translate "daily" is not found elsewhere. Origen thought it to be an original coinage. It may be translated "of the coming day."

[8] Martin Luther insisted that daily bread means "everything necessary to the support and comfort of existence, as food and raiment, house and land, money and goods, a kind spouse, good children, faithful servants, righteous magistrates, good weather, peace, health, honor, true friends, good neighbors, and the like."

great the struggle to obtain sufficient food has been for most of the human beings who have ever lived, and even for millions today who survive on the narrowest of margins. Because we live in an economy of abundance, in which we are embarrassed by our growing surplus of most things, we are likely to forget how uncharacteristic this situation is. For the majority of our ancestors, the adage "If a man will not work, neither can he eat" was the very essence of human experience. Survival through the winter, with the storage of sufficient fuel and food, was almost always a major problem. Now, in spite of increased production, the enormous rise in population makes this a continuing problem in many sectors of the globe.

Even in affluence the prayer for daily bread is still relevant, partly because of the plural number of the pronoun. The prayer is for "us," not merely for "me." Here is a logical continuation of Matthew's opening, "Our Father." When Christianity is true to its fundamental insights, there is always a movement from the singular to the plural, in that the basic requests are for others and not for ourselves alone. And however prosperous we may become, finite man is never independent of his physical base. The prayer for food may logically be extended to prayer for health, for recovery from illness and for strength, because hunger, pain, and sickness are mankind's common enemies. When we pray for bread we are entering consciously into the fellowship of those who bear the mark of hunger.

The fourth request is for forgiveness. This is the most nearly universal request of all, since we cannot imagine a situation in which it is not relevant. It is conceivable that there may one day be enough food for all, but it is not conceivable that we should not need to ask to be forgiven. The recognition of this fact is what makes the General Confession so appropriate in services of public worship. In so far as we are honest at all, we can recognize that we have been disloyal to the moral demand, if not in deed, at least in thought.

What requires forgiveness is not, primarily, deeds done, but deeds not done. We have reason to be heartily ashamed for words of encouragement not said and for powers never developed. Robert Louis Stevenson understood the human situation clearly at this point. In his famous essay, "A Christmas Sermon," Stevenson wrote, "We are not damned for doing wrong, but for not doing right." Lovers of Stevenson's prayers may remember how his widow tells, in her beautiful introduction to *Prayers Written at Vailima*, of his leaving the company one night, before they had said the "Our Father." Shocked and angered at having recently heard of an example of unexpected treachery on the part of one in whom he had every reason to trust, he arose as the singing stopped and abruptly left the room. His wife, fearing illness, hastened after him to ask the reason for his sudden departure. "It is this," he replied, "I am not yet fit to say, 'Forgive us our trespasses as we forgive those who trespass against us.'"

If it is recognition of failure to act that most clearly makes us conscious of the need to be forgiven, the recognition comes most vividly in connection with those who are closest to us. "Worst of all," says Dean Coburn, "you remember hurting the people you love most, and turning your back on so many opportunities to show them your love."[9]

The clear teaching of the Church on forgiveness is shown by the fact that it is listed, as one specific item, in the Apostles' Creed. Belief in "The Forgiveness of Sins" is emphasized equally along with the "Holy Ghost," "The holy Catholic Church," "The Communion of Saints," "The Resurrection of the body," "And the Life everlasting." This is really very remarkable, since these, on the surface, do not seem to be of equal importance. No doubt the emphasis upon forgiveness in the Pattern Prayer was one of the reasons for this accentuation of the theme. The Nicene Creed does not employ this particular expression, though it does connect the "remission

[9] *Prayer and Personal Religion, op. cit.*, p. 20.

of sins" with baptism. Of the two great creeds, the Apostles' Creed is the one that is far closer to the simplicity of the Pattern Prayer.

By using the simple word "sins," Luke is probably closer to the original than is Matthew with his "debts," but the similarity of meaning is close. It is unfortunate that in modern Christendom, what ought to be a uniting prayer is sometimes a divisive one, in that different churches use different words at the crucial point. Presbyterians, for example, tend to say "debts," while Episcopalians, Methodists, and others say "trespasses." The result is that many persons lapse into silence when they reach the forgiveness cause, for bear of being in conflict with surrounding persons. If all could go back to Luke's version and unite on the direct word "sins," this would constitute an important steps in ecumenicity. The attraction of the word "sin" consists in the fact that it is easily understood and is highly applicable to our lives, whereas the word "trespasses" may be neglected because it is antique.

Both versions involve the forgiveness of others as a condition of our own forgiveness. Matthew goes even further, in this regard, by adding a postscript, as though the matter had not already been made sufficiently clear: "For if you forgive others the wrongs they have done, your heavenly Father will also forgive you; but if you do not forgive others, then the wrongs you have done will not be forgiven by your Father" (6:14-15, NEB). Our relationship to God is conditioned by our relationship to men. Bitterness is a barrier!

Here is something very similar to Kant's categorical imperative, since it is based ultimately upon the principle of consistency. Why make exceptions of ourselves? Is there any reason why I should be forgiven more than others, since we are in a common human predicament? Therefore, if I am consistent, I shall apply to all others the very standard which I want to have applied to myself, and, if I do not apply the standard to others, I have no right to expect that it should be applied to me. My duty is to ask that my maxim apply to myself only in so far as it has already been consciously universalized.

Though the idea is surprising to many, it is possible that there is a touch of humor in this request. A man who is taught to ask that he be forgiven *as* he had forgiven others may learn to laugh at his own pretensions when he suddenly realizes what poor forgiveness this would be! The idea is at least potentially humorous in that it enables us to prick the bubble of our self-righteousness and to see ourselves with some objectivity. In many instances, we have to admit that if our own forgiveness is *similar* to what we give out to others, *there won't be any at all!* Who is there among us who can claim that he does not nourish animosities and harbor grudges? The prayer, then, turns out to be a marvelous instrument of self-examination. The best laughter is a quiet one, directed at ourselves.

Sinners we undoubtedly are, but the wonderful fact is that we *can* be sinners forgiven. Forgiveness, which means a brand new start without wasting moral energy on grieving over past offenses, is essential to the picture of God as Father. If this is how a good earthly parent deals with a child, how much more is it God's way of dealing with the immature beings we call human. There is no way of overemphasizing the healing effect of this conception. Sins, then, are neither ignored nor dwelt upon. "It is right," says Dean Coburn, "to be concerned with our sins. It is wrong to be obsessed by them."[10] The Christian community survives and thrives, not as the fellowship of the righteous, but as the fellowship of the mutually forgiven, because divinely forgiven. There can be no Church without confession. This is what Luther meant when he said, in the *Large Catechism*, "Therefore when I admonish you to confession I am admonishing you to be a Christian."

However helpful the psychiatrist may sometimes prove to be, the approach to sin in the Christian context is far more profound. The psychiatrist seems to be above in the battle,

[10] *Ibid.*, p. 42.

but the Christian brother shares in the confession. "In the presence of a psychiatrist," says Bonhoeffer, "I can only be a sick man; in the presence of a Christian brother, I can dare to be a sinner."[11] A man enters a Christian fellowship, not on a couch, but on his knees, and he faces others who are also on their knees. Herein is the ultimate realism which comes by looking at ourselves without face-saving deceit. "Whoever," said Doctor Johnson, "considers the weakness both of himself and others, will not long want persuasives to forgiveness."[12]

Hard as it may be to forgive, when we tend to cherish our grudge, it is actually harder to *ask* for forgiveness, because this is an act which represents an ultimate break in the façade of a man's self-esteem. There is a sense in which forgiveness of others can make us feel magnanimous and generous, and thus there is moral danger, even in doing what is right, whereas asking for forgiveness makes for intrinsic humility. Seldom in a man's life is he actually nobler than when he says, "I was wrong; I am ashamed; please forgive me." Perhaps this is why more of the words of Christ's Pattern Prayer are devoted to this subject than to any other. Since the root of sin is pride, public confession is basic; it strikes at the root.

The final petition of the Pattern Prayer has often been confusing to serious and devout Christians. Many admit that when they say "And lead us not into temptation," they find it hard to make this consistent with Christ's picture of the Father. The notion that God, in fact, ever leads us deliberately into temptation is shocking, but it seems to many to be implied in the fact that we ask that this should not occur. The problem is harder in Luke's version, for there "Lead us not into temptation" has no balancing and clarifying clause, as is found in Matthew 6:13.

There are several considerations that can help us in this felt difficulty. One is the translation provided by the scholars who have produced *The New English Bible*, which is "And

[11] Dietrich Bonhoeffer, *Life Together*, translated by John W. Doberstein (New York: Harper & Row, 1954), p. 119.
[12] Samuel Johnson, *The Rambler*, Christmas Eve, 1751.

do not bring us to the test." The word translated "temptation" may also be translated "trial" or "test," and this meaning seems to be substantiated by the parallel "But deliver us from evil." Matthew provides this balance of two sentences, saying the same thing in a slightly different and therefore clarifying form. This literary form is similar to the parallelism of Hebrew poetry, with which we are familiar in the Psalms. Thus "The earth is the Lord's" is balanced and amplified by another statement, "and the fulness thereof," while there is an obvious parallelism between "The heavens declare the glory of God" and "The firmament showeth his handiwork." We are fortunate in the fact that Matthew's version has preserved this sort of parallel statement in the last part of the Pattern Prayer because it helps to solve the problem which many sincerely feel.

The average reader will be aided by realizing that the question is not the one he fears, viz., the question whether God deliberately sends temptation. The request is that hard-pressed men may be saved from tests which are too difficult for them, just as they may be saved from debilitating hunger. What Christ emphasizes is that hard tests will come. The gospel inevitably involves suffering and all must learn to bear the cross daily. The Christian pilgrimage is not the ordinary story of success, and those who cannot drink the bitter cup are warned to stay away from it. Never do we find Christ begging any to join, but we do find Him issuing warnings concerning the high cost of apostleship.

Even after men understand that Christ calls to hardship, there could be some tests that would be too hard to bear. Here we are given a preview of the Gethsemane scene. The Pattern Prayer gives the first hint of "let this cup pass from me" (Matt. 26:39). The temptation mentioned in the Pattern Prayer is not something deliberately placed before men in order to assist in the building of athletic strength. The temptations mentioned are not, in short, artifically contrived, but are, instead, the fierce hardships which are inherent in living in this cruel world. If we appreciate truly our own weakness, it is reasonable to pray that we be spared those ultimate tests in the face of which no one can stand. The experiences of men and women in prison camps during World War II make each of us wonder if there are tortures which we simply could not bear. It is extremely realistic to end our prayer, not with the request that our lives should follow rose-strewn paths, but simply that they not be too hard. It is an honest estimate of human weakness.

The inclusion of a reference to temptation in the "Our Father" is supported by abundant reference to the same subject elsewhere in the gospel record. In the moving account of the experience in the Garden of Gethsemane, temptation is emphasized by being mentioned twice, as follows: "And when he came to the place he said to them, 'Pray that you may not enter into temptation'" (Luke 22:40), and "Rise and pray that you may not enter into temptation" (Luke 22:46). Mark and Matthew make the second reference to temptation even more vivid by quoting Christ's admonition as follows: "Watch and pray that you may not enter into temptation" (Mark 14:38 and Matt. 26:41). Here is the very best commentary on the fifth petition of the Pattern Prayer, for it is Christ's own.

A major truth concerning temptation is that when temptation comes, it is usually already too late. The decision whether or not to yield to temptation has already been deeply influenced by prior decisions, and by prior preparations for moral defense. Unless we arm ourselves in advance of the moral battle, we have very little chance when finally the actual test occurs. In this, as in so much else that involves depth of insight, we can follow Professor John Baillie. He saw that watching and praying overlapped, because " Prayer is *the soul's vigil.*" Our best chance of escape from moral danger (and even this is not absolute) lies in the act of prayerful preparedness. "So it is that sin is conquered," said Professor Baillie, "not in the moment of temptation but in the long prayerful discipline that precedes it."[13] The fifth and final petition of the Pattern Prayer is thus intensely practical in that it leads to a way of getting ready. We cannot know what the particular test will be today or tomorrow, but we can be sure that it will often be hard, and that we are not so rich in moral resources that we can reasonably neglect the greatest of these, prayer itself. The acme of Christian wisdom lies in the succinct statement, "Therefore, you also must be ready" (Matt. 24:44).

We have called the "Our Father" the Pattern Prayer because this seems to be less confusing than is the ordinary term by which we refer to it, yet even this involves danger. We must not think of the prayer as representing a fixed pattern. Buttrick is probably right in calling it a "type." It must be seen, not as a new devotional bondage, but as a form which leads to liberation. All of the particular petitions must be construed broadly if we are to do justice to the typical prayer, which is appropriate for finite souls. When we say "Our Father who art in heaven" we should not thereby suggest that He is not on earth! When we say "Thy kingdom come" we must not let ourselves be fettered by some dogmatic eschatological conception. The great prayer is a point from which to start, not a fixed terminus.

Part of the greatness of the Pattern Prayer lies in the fact that it is so mundane at the same time that it is dignified. It shows that we do not have to speak to God in "religious" language or confine ourselves to "spiritual" matters. The petition for bread takes care of that. Furthermore, the prayer does not argue. Underlying it all is the ultimate conviction expressed by "My Father is working still, and I am working" (John 5:17). The more we meditate on this prayer which our Lord suggested to His followers, including ourselves, the more we see the soundness of the late Archbishop Temple's conclusion, "It is the prayer you would want to offer if you loved God with all your heart."[14]

[13] *Christian Devotion, op. cit.,* p. 58.

[14] William Temple, *Christian Faith and Life* (London: Student Christian Movement Press, 1957), p. 111.

CHAPTER IV

⋯⧢⧣⋯

Prayer for a Labor Force

"Pray therefore the Lord of the harvest to
send out laborers into his harvest."
Luke 10:2

E VEN WHEN WE RECOGNIZE that Christ uttered and suggested several prayers, we tend to suppose that these are in some sense decorations added to the total account, and that their omission would not involve any serious loss. The more we meditate, however, the more we realize that such is not the case. The prayers are vitally necessary if the rest of the story is to be understood with any adequacy. The prayers which Christ uttered help us greatly in our effort to understand His relation to the Father, while the prayers suggested or commanded for His followers help equally in the understanding of the nature of the Christian movement as a whole.

Although we recognize, when we think about the matter, that the prayer conventionally termed the Lord's Prayer is for the followers and is not Christ's own devotional utterance, we do not always realize that there is another prayer which He asked those who were His associates to employ. We have it in a very brief form, but its importance is obvious, partly because it appears twice and in very different contexts, once in Matthew 9:38 and again in Luke 10:2. Here Christ does not tell, as He told on other occasions, *how* to pray or how *not* to pray, but rather what to pray *for*. He says to pray for the recruitment or enlistment of *workers*. It is the conviction of a growing group of scholars, of whom Professor Vartan Melconian of McCormick Theological Seminary is one, that in this proposed prayer lies one of the most significant keys to the entire understanding of the nature of the gospel.

The fact that Christ asked for a particular prayer twice does not necessarily indicate that the two authors have arbitrarily placed the command in settings convenient to their narrative. It is logically possible that Christ said this once in the setting provided by Matthew and again in the setting provided by Luke, for both make sense. Indeed, it is wholly reasonable to suppose that Christ commanded this prayer many times, though only two instances were recorded. Repetition of the same words in different situations is an intelligent procedure and a good teaching device.

Luke's introduction of the injunction to pray for the growth of a labor force is associated with the sending out of the Seventy.[1] This incident, which is unique to Luke's account, presumably refers to a second missionary circle, perhaps less highly trained than the Twelve, but employed, like the Twelve, to serve as shock troops in penetrating surrounding society. The key explanation is that "the Lord appointed seventy others, and sent them on ahead of him, two by two, into every town and place where he himself was about to come" (10:1). Since these people, thus sent, were by no stretch of the imagination religious professionals, the passage which this sentence introduces has come to be a favorite one with many who are devoted to the concept of the lay ministry. The members of this larger band were charged with much of the same stern discipline that was required of the Twelve. They were told that they would not be popular, that they were, indeed, sheep among wolves, and that they were not to expect luxuries (Matt. 10:9-16). They were not to loiter, because the task was an urgent one, and, accordingly, they were not to waste time on those who were unwilling to listen.

[1] Possibly seventy-two. This number is used in *The New English Bible*.

The upshot is that the Seventy were to pray for the emergence of a task force and also were to be a partial answer to their own prayer by *becoming* such a force. They were one means by which the ministry of Christ was multiplied. There is every reason to suppose that they were expected to return to their common lives after completing their special effort, and it is wholly credible that they went out more than once. After all, only a fraction of the gospel story was ever recorded.

The most remarkable feature of the entire event, as recorded, was the stunning success of this venture in lay missionary activity. They found, apparently to their surprise, that people *did* listen, and that mental healings actually occurred. "Lord," they said, "even the demons are subject to us in your name!" Refreshing as this result is, the most important feature is Christ's own estimate of the success of the experiment. "And he said to them, 'I saw Satan fall like lightning from heaven'" (Luke 10:17-18). There is no other statement in the entire gospel record which exceeds this in hopefulness. He seems to say that in the use of the devoted amateur, rightly motivated and rightly trained, is a method that can win. The effectiveness of such a group is in marked contrast to the effectiveness of religious professionals. It was as though He had meditated long on the way to achieve a genuine breakthrough and at last He had found it. Here was a method which the forces of evil could not withstand. The very gates of hell could not resist the penetration of this kind of Church.

The other setting of the injunction to pray for the rise of a labor force makes the meaning even more clear. Matthew makes it his introduction to the appointment of the Twelve, which, as we have already seen, constitutes a dividing line in Christ's public ministry. This was the immense change from emphasis on disciples to emphasis on apostles. We must remember that the disciples were already numerous, but their effect seems to have been slight, because they were primarily listeners rather than doers. What had already been done was no doubt a good preparation, but it was not enough. Christ could heal and reach a few, but some method was needed to accomplish far more.

It was, Matthew tells us, the sight of the confused crowds of people that impelled our Lord to find a new method. They seemed to Him to lack direction and purpose, even though there was much good in them that was potential. They were, most accurately, sheep without a shepherd. Who has not felt this in contact with modern crowds? There is so much that *could* be done, but the problem is that of finding adequate and devoted developers of other people's powers. Often people are ready to study, but where are the teachers to be found? In this matching of hope and failure Christ declared, "The harvest is plentiful, but the laborers are few" (Matt. 9:37).

In Matthew's sequence, this bold statement of the central paradox of opportunity and failure led directly to the prayer for the recruitment of workers, and then to the selection of the key workers, the Twelve, who were later sent out. The logical development is perfect, even though the record is severely condensed. We must note that the whole conception is based upon the conviction that the time had come for harvest and not merely for *sowing*. The inference is that many among the harassed crowds are more nearly ready for a new life than they themselves realize. There are deep desires for wholeness that are not fully articulated, but which could be harvested rapidly, if only there were the right people to undertake the task with the requisite skill. Nothing of any consequence can occur until people are ready, but people may be more nearly ready than they ordinarily suppose. We seldom have to do as much preparatory work as we think we must. "Do you not say, 'There are yet four months, then comes the harvest'? I tell you, lift up your eyes, and see how the fields are already white for harvest" (John 4:35).

When we face squarely the fact that Christ asked His followers, including us, to pray for a labor force, many other features of the gospel begin to take on new significance, and the familiar figures of speech come alive. Metaphorical allusions to fishing, to sheep herding and to plowing, all fall into place and the great figure of the yoke assumes central importance. The major point to get straight is that *Christ did not ask for admirers*, but rather for workers in His cause. Because halfhearted or merely sentimental followers are not helpful, Christ actually tried to dissuade them. What other meaning can be given to His apparent effort to check the enthusiasm of a volunteer by referring to the fact that "the Son of man has nowhere to lay his head" (Luke 9:58)? It was because of those who wished to be disciples, but not to be fully employed laborers, that Christ made His famous allusion to plowing. "No one who puts his hand to the plow and looks back is fit for the kingdom of God" (Luke 9:62). This metaphor is so meaningful that some men of one Protestant group have worn lapel buttons in the shape of a small plow. It is a way of their reminding themselves that they are called to engage in a task, rather than merely to attend meetings.

The request for prayer, which we are considering, also makes the original call of Simon and Andrew more significant. To follow meant to be *employed*. "And passing along by the Sea of Galilee, he saw Simon and Andrew the brother of Simon casting a net into the sea; for they were fishermen. And Jesus said to them 'Follow me and I will make you become fishers of men'" (Mark 1:16-17). The call was not to a contemplative life nor to a mystical experience, for their own comfort and enjoyment, and no reference was made to worship. The call was, from the start, a call to missionary activity. These men were Christ's first followers and the direction of their task was outward from its very inception.

All of this comes to a climax, in Matthew 11:29-30, in the famous reference to Christ's yoke. Again, the impetus is provided by the sight of the harassed and leaderless multitudes, living in confusion, when life could be creatively directed. The tragedy of waste seems to have touched Christ deeply as He contemplated the contrast between the potential and the actual in most human lives. Those whose lot concerned Him, then, were the people whose work was hard and whose load was heavy. But the problem was not that men had to work; the problem was the purposelessness of the work. "It is using a pick-axe to no purpose that makes a prison," said Saint-Exupéry. The paradox of Christ's answer to the toiling and frustrated populace was not surcease from labor, but work in a new context. We all see this when we realize that the yoke, if it means anything at all, means an instrument of labor. It is a kind of harness by which loads are carried or plows pulled.

When Christ said "Take my yoke upon you, and learn from me" (Matt. 11:29), He was uttering the clearest call to commitment which He is known as having made in His entire public ministry. One of the good things about the development of the Christian faith in our generation is the emphasis upon commitment, an emphasis which we owe partly to the rise of existentialism. The renewed importance of this aspect of the gospel is indicated by the fact that the yoke has come to be a much more familiar symbol in our generation and that Matthew 11:29 is now, for many thoughtful people, the favorite text of the entire Bible.

What is abundantly clear, then, is that Christ was not offering a panacea which could, by any stretch of the imagination, he considered cheap grace. He was not offering peace of mind, as is ordinarily understood, but by contrast said, as though to correct a misunderstanding, "You must not think that I have come to bring peace . . . but a sword" (Matt. 10:34, NEB). The good news was therefore hard and costly, and might unfortunately divide families rather than unite them. This is a sad phenomenon which we have observed in our own time. Above all, what Christ proposed in order to give meaning to the meaningless lives was not ease or entertainment, but enlistment in a labor corps, along with the reverent prayer that others should be added to the corps. Life is not made good by retirement or by mere leisure, but always by finding some task into which men can throw themselves so fully that they forget to concentrate either upon their present aches and pains or upon their past disappointments and sins. The man holding the handle of the plow must always look forward. Only in this way can he expect to plow a reasonably straight furrow.

If we were to take seriously Christ's prayer for a labor force and apply it to ourselves, we should make a much closer connection between prayer and daily work than is ordinarily made. We tend to think that prayer is an alternative to work, which it certainly is not. We owe to John Baillie one of the clearest statements of the proper relation between work and prayer. It appears in his posthumously printed sermon, "To Pray and not to Faint," a sermon based on Luke 18:1. The text is "And he spake a parable unto them to this end, that men ought always to pray, and not to faint" (AV). Dr. Baillie's fresh insight is the recognition that the word "faint" as an alternative to prayer comes to the average reader as a surprise.

We are so apt to interpret the meaning of prayer as if Jesus had said that men ought always to pray and not to *work*. That, I believe, is precisely the mistake that most of us make in our thinking about prayer: we think of it as an alternative to effort. We often speak as if there were two contrasted ways of facing the evils of our mortal lot—we may either fold our hands and pray about them, or we may pull ourselves together and do what we can to mend them. And standing as we do in the tradition of what the philosophers call Western activism you and I are almost sure to regard the latter as the nobler and manlier way.[2]

There is no doubt that Dr. Baillie is right about our normal presuppositions, but it is likewise clear that our normal presuppositions are wrong. At least they are inconsistent with the teaching and practice of Christ. "He regarded prayer," writes Baillie, "not as an alternative to effort, but as an accom-

[2] *Christian Devotion, op. cit.,* p. 44.

paniment of effort and an alternative to despairing acquiscence and inaction." The consequence of Christ's teaching is that working is not the opposite of praying; its true contrary is doing nothing at all. It is frequently the same set of men and women who work most tirelessly for a cause and also pray most continuously. Prayer, for Jesus, is not connected with resignation, after the Stoic pattern.

It is part of the glory of the prayer life of that rough and brilliant man, Doctor Samuel Johnson, that the finest of his written prayers are connected with daily work. We have about a hundred of his prayers, most of them deposited in his own handwriting at his old college in Oxford, and the final one, the last thing the great man ever wrote, in the library at Yale. Johnson saw his secular and practical studies, not as something apart from his religion, but as the chief forms which his religion could take. Though a dictionary is as secular as a literary work can be, Johnson saw the herculean task of composing one as the sacred work to which God had called him. Writing it, laborious as this task was, was his way of making sure that his divinely given talents were not wasted. The prayer on *The Dictionary* is as follows:

O God, who hast hitherto supported me, enable me to proceed in this labour, and in the whole task of my present state; that when I shall render up, at the last day, an account of the talent committed to me, I may receive pardon, for the sake of Jesus Christ. Amen.[3]

Johnson's prayer on *The Rambler* is well known, since it appears in Boswell's *Life of Johnson*, but many do not know equally well the really remarkable prayer on *The Study of Law*.

Almighty God, the Giver of Wisdom, without whose help resolutions are vain, without whose blessing study is ineffectual, enable me, if it be thy will, to attain such knowledge as may qualify me to direct the doubtful, and instruct the ignorant, to prevent wrongs, and terminate contentions; and grant that I may use that knowl-

[3] *Doctor Johnson's Prayers* (New York: Harper & Row, 1947), p. 8.

edge which I shall attain, to thy glory and my own salvation, for Jesus Christ's sake. Amen.[4]

In his inspired and inspiring connection between prayer and toil, Johnson was being loyal to the teaching of William Law, whose *Serious Call* he had read while a student at Oxford. He expected the book to be dull or to be something about which he could laugh, but he was honest enough to make another judgment when he actually read the book. "I found," he said, "Law quite an overmatch for me." What the famous lexicographer got from Law, above all, was the notion of the possible unification of prayer and common life. Law advised special times of prayer and thus followed his Lord, but the devout man, he wrote, is he "who considers and serves God in everything and who makes all of his life an act of devotion by doing everything in the name of God and under such rules as are comfortable to His glory."[5]

The whole literature of private prayer is enriched by the idea, whenever it appears, that prayer and work go together as Christ taught. Thus, one of the most appealing of the prayers of Robert Louis Stevenson in Samoa, is one used in the morning as he faced, with his helpers, the labor of the day.

The day returns and brings us the petty round of irritating concerns and duties. Help us to play the man, help us to perform them with laughter and kind faces, let cheerfulness abound with industry. Give us to go blithely on our business all this day, bring us to our resting beds weary and content and undishonoured, and grant us in the end the gift of sleep.[6]

The fact that Christ asked men for a labor force means, among other things, that this was something which He greatly desired and that He wanted His followers to understand. Because he was proposing something fundamentally new, He engaged, necessarily, in the arduous task of trying to make people

[4] *Ibid.*, p. 10.
[5] *Op. cit.*, p. 17.
[6] *Prayers Written at Vailima*, available in many editions.

understand what it was that was proposed. There are many evidences that even the closest followers did not get the idea fully. If they had, James and John would not have argued about personal status for themselves, working through their mother, and the Apostles would not have supposed, at the end, that Christ's purpose was political. "Lord," they asked, "will you at this time restore the kingdom to Israel?" (Acts 1:6).

In order to give some idea of the novelty of His vision for the Church, Christ had to say, on the one hand, what the Church was *not*. Thus, in the twelfth chapter of Matthew we find, three times, the expression "greater than," applied once to the Temple and all its ceremonial restrictions (12:6), once to prophetic preaching, "Something greater than Jonah is here," (12:41), and again to worldly wisdom, "Something greater than Solomon is here" (12:42). Whether He was referring to Himself or to His Church as that which was greater, makes little difference, since His Church was the historical extension of Himself. He was forced, first of all, to distinguish the new thing that was emerging from all those elements of religion with which men naturally tended to identify or confuse it.

On the positive side, Christ employed numerous metaphors in the obvious attempt to make clear something that was not understood at all or was dimly seen. To this end He compared the new movement to salt, and light, and leaven, all of which are marked by the penetration of that which surrounds them. In this way the connection between the new fellowship and the world was variously suggested. What should, therefore, have been obvious was that the new movement, though deeply religious in one sense, was, at the same time, in marked contrast to what most people thought religion entailed. One of the sharpest contrasts lay in the attempted erasure of the distinction between the sacred and the secular, with the consequence that the major locus of the Church was the world.

The salt was the salt of the *earth*; the light was the light of the *world*; the conflagration that Christ proposed to kindle was to set fire to the *earth* (Luke 12:49).[7]

One of the saddest features of subsequent Christian history has been the tendency to fall back into pre-Christian conceptions of how the love of God is to be best expressed. Thus, though the entire New Testament mentions not one single shrine, Christians have set up many shrines, always with some encouragement to superstition. Christ's clear teaching is that of the universality of His real presence, *wherever* two or three are gathered, but His supposed followers have frequently claimed that His presence is more real at some places than at others. The lesson of absolute humility, taught by washing the feet of His followers, is constantly rejected by emphasis upon ecclesiastical status, including insistence on honorific titles. The idolatry of the building harks back, before Christ, to the glorification of the Temple, and much of our liturgical revival is concerned with matters which Christ outmoded. He ridiculed those who were meticulous about religious clothing (Matt. 23:5).

Of all of the ways in which we, who claim to be Christ's followers, are commonly pre-Christian, the most striking is our supposition that we do our Christian duty by sitting in "audiences." It is easy to find great numbers who think that they can fulfill their Christian responsibility by doing two things: first, attending a few "services" in which they listen to sermons; and, second, giving a little money to support those who are doing Christ's work in the modern world, either at home or abroad. The performance of these two minimal tasks normally produces an easy conscience. Often a pastor is counted successful if he can get the members to do these two things, especially if their contributions improve the church building. The following, taken from a contemporary newspaper, tells about a successful pastor:

[7] For a contemporary expression of this fundamental conception see *Where in the World*, by Colin W. Williams (New York: National Council of the Churches of Christ in the U. S. A., 1963).

During the ministry of X, $68,319 was spent for buildings and improvements. The sanctuary has been completely renovated; new light fixtures, rugs, pew cushions and air conditioning have been added in the sanctuary, and the social hall has been redecorated. A new console was provided for the sanctuary, and a sprinkler system installed on the lawn. Two parking lots were paved.

In another part of the news article we are told that the clergyman who has promoted all this local comfort is also interested in foreign missions. There is, of course, much merit in giving to foreign missions, as there is much merit in making a building beautiful. Not even air conditioning is intrinsically evil, though overconcern for our own personal comfort certainly is. The important thing to make clear is that the ordinary tests of Christian success, of which the above newspaper account is not a caricature, are far from the tests of Christ. They are not bad, but they are not central, and they are, in no sense, distinctively Christian.

In the average church of our day, emphasis is placed upon worship. Great energy is expended on the effort to provide people with an atmosphere conducive to worship and to encourage people to take advantage of it. For most people, "going to church" now means, not the task of learning how to be a lay evangelist nor even teaching a class, but attendance at public worship. What is required is that people sit in pews, share in responses, sing hymns, listen to the choir's anthems, and pay close attention to both the prayers and the preaching of the pastor. The hope is that the people so gathered will have an emotional experience which involves a sense of reverence. It is for this purpose that the main structure of a modern church building is constructed. This is why it is now standard to have a divided chancel, with emphasis on a beautiful altar with rich appointments. The heart of the church building is now supposed to be a "worship center."

However good this is, it is in sharp contrast to anything commanded by Christ and to the dominant mood of the New Testament. Even though he wrote it more than two hundred years ago, it is still a little shocking to read the passage from William Law in which he makes this point clear.

It is very observable that there is not one command in all the Gospels for public worship. The frequent attendance at it is never so much as mentioned in all the New Testament. On the other hand, our blessed Savior and his apostles are wholly taken up in doctrines that relate to every day life. . . . Is it not exceedingly strange, therefore, that people should place so much emphasis upon attendance at public worship—concerning which there is not one precept of our Lord's to be found—and yet neglect these common duties of our ordinary life which are commanded in every page of the Gospels?[8]

Neither Law nor those of our day who are influenced by him can rightly be said to oppose regular worship. What is rejected is the notion that worship is central or sufficient.

In establishing a balance, Christ's call to prayer as recorded in Luke 10:2 and Matthew 9:38 becomes positively significant. That He envisaged a fellowship is perfectly clear. There is not even a suggestion of the sort of experience reflected in the practice of the ancient Athenians as they went, one by one, to the Parthenon to offer their votive gifts to the goddess. Likewise, there is no similarity to what occurs even today at a Shinto shrine. Christ did not come to bring another version of one-by-one religion. But when we see that He desired the fellowship, which we might reasonably call the congregation, we dare not stop there. A congregation can be gathered for many reasons. It can be gathered to watch jointly a performance, to hear an address, or to pray in common. Much of this was already practiced in the synogogue which Christ rejected and which, on at least one significant occasion, rejected Him (Luke 4:16-30).

The repeated call to prayer tells what the fellowship is for. It is for *toil*, for working in the harvest field of the world. The unavoidable conclusion is that Christ saw the emerging Church, which was required if the world were to be saved

[8] *Op. cit.*, pp. 18, 19.

from decay, as a *missionary band*. In this sense it was to be radically different from the Temple, with its periodic celebrations and sacrifices, and it was to be likewise different from the synagogue, where the congregation was audience. The best thing that could be said of those in the synagogue was that they were disciples, but this is radically different from being apostles.

Christ's third way, which the repeated call to prayer helps to delineate, was the formation of an apostolic band. Whenever, in any denomination today, an effort is made to revive the "lay apostolate," the suggested prayer is in some measure being answered. The Church, when it takes seriously the prayer in question, is highly missionary, but not missionary merely in the sense that it raises budgets to *send* missionaries and to maintain missionary offices in large cities. It is missionary in the deeper sense that all of the members *are* missionaries, each finding how to make his witness in the common life to which God has called him.

To pray that God will send forth laborers is to recognize that the essence of the Church is mission. There ought to be times when people listen to sermons, but this is not our major task; it is only one *preparation* for our task. The "service" is in the world, not in the church building, but what transpires in the church building may serve to increase the effectiveness of that service.

We can rightly be attentive to those who, particularly in our time, have emphasized the idea of the Church as a "gathered fellowship," sometimes called "The Household of Faith." The very word "ecumenical" is reminiscent of the separated household. But we dare not stop with the idea of gathering or of being called out of the world, for this is only part of the total pattern. We are indeed gathered, but we are gathered in order to be scattered. We come in, it is true, but we come in in order to go out. The gathering of the workers is in order that they may be briefed for their task, and also may gain strength from one another to keep going when the task is arduous. The

Church of Jesus Christ must be both gathered and scattered, both *ecclesia* and *diaspora*. The East German Working Group of the World Council of Churches, a group which makes its witness under exceedingly difficult circumstances, reports the experience "that the congregation is truly Christian when it is seen as a gathering which takes place 'for the purpose of sending.'"[9]

What is really amazing is the degree to which the suggested prayer was answered in the early Church. The members seemed to sense that they were called to something very different from the religious expectations of the peoples whose life they penetrated. Their approach was so novel that the Stoic and Epicurean philosophers of Athens, who were accustomed to new ideas, were plainly mystified. The Greeks who brought Paul to the Areopagus said, not very surprisingly, "May we know what this new teaching is which you present? For you bring some strange things to our ears" (Acts 17:19-20).

What went on at Athens, and at many other places in the Greek world, as well as in Rome, *was* "strange," and it was strange, in part, because here was a movement in which all were workers. Some were naturally more gifted than others, and leaders will emerge in any movement, but all the evidence that we have points to the conclusion that in the early Christian fellowship, member and missionary or evangelist were equivalent terms!

Modern man is likely to miss the wide employment of military metaphors in the New Testament, partly because he thinks of this use as merely poetical or hopelessly antique. But the more we ponder, the more we realize the extreme appropriateness of such vivid language. The workers were organized along military lines, in the sense that a man might be sent anywhere at any time, in a battle which was wideranging. A recent Presbyterian comment on this theme is clarifying:

[9] *Where in the World, op. cit.*, p. 97.

The New Testament word for "order" (tassö) came from military parlance. It was the term used for the swift deployment of a fighting unit from a marching to a battle formation. . . . Order is the Church readying itself, moving out on its mission, in obedience to the sovereign God. Different campaigns in the life of the Church may call for different tactics, and a quite different ordering. . . . On every level, and at every stage, order has a single purpose: *to enable the Church to deploy its forces most effectively in its assigned mission in and for the world.*[10]

When Christ, then, bade us pray that God should send laborers into the harvest, He was bidding us pray for the Church, for that is what the Church is. It is a band of shock troops; it is a labor battalion; it is a company of harvesters. No place exists in it for the observer or for the mere supporter. There are no passengers on the sacred ship, because all are in the crew.

Such was the dream, never fully realized and never wholly forgotten. It was and is highly disturbing to our complacency about our relative success. Whenever it is seriously adopted, events which are miraculous occur, in which the penetration, though never complete, goes on at great speed. The Church, which is both our hope and our despair, never wholly succeeds and never wholly fails, but it is always glorified by the dream which possesses it. We should not really understand this dream if we did not pay careful attention to what Christ asks. The request for prayer for recruits is, Glover suggests, "perhaps the only place where he asked his disciples to pray for his great work."[11] The prayer involved in this request is particularly important, because it is the one prayer which He most clearly commanded.

[10] *The Church and Its Changing Ministry*, edited by R. C. Johnson (Philadelphia: United Presbyterian Church, 1962), pp. 20, 21.
[11] T. R. Glover, *The Jesus of History* (New York: The Association Press, 1917), p. 111.

CHAPTER V

✺

The Personal Prayer

> "I thank thee, Father."
> *Matthew* 11:25

THUS FAR WE HAVE devoted our attention to Christ's practice
of prayer, to His teaching about prayer, and to two prayers
which He suggested that others should pray. Now, throughout
the remainder of this book, we can give full attention to those
prayers which our Lord Himself is known to have prayed.
The first of these, and one of the most revealing, is very short.
Though it is not mentioned in Mark, it appears in almost
identical form in both Matthew and Luke, in different settings. Most scholars, who believe that before the actual writing
of any of our Gospels there existed a collection of sayings of
Christ, are convinced that the passage which highlights the
first of the recorded prayers is from this collection. This collection of sayings, which may go back to eye-witnesses and to
original hearers of the words of Christ, and is normally called
Q, from the German *Quelle*, "source," was apparently not
known to Mark, but it was available to Matthew and Luke,
who seem to have used it freely. The evidence of such use is
best recognized by studying the Synoptic Gospels in three
parallel columns.[1]

Because the passage mentioned probably reflects the eye-

[1] A contemporary volume which makes this easily possible is *Gospel Parallels*
(New York: Thomas Nelson & Sons, 1957).

witness account and because it deals with matters of supreme importance, we should look at it in full. The account in Luke, which comes immediately after the triumphant return of the Seventy, is as follows:

> In that same hour he rejoiced in the Holy Spirit and said, "I thank thee, Father, Lord of heaven and earth, that thou hast hidden these things from the wise and understanding and revealed them to babes; yea, Father, for such was thy gracious will. All things have been delivered to me by my Father; and no one knows who the Son is except the Father, or who the Father is except the Son and any one to whom the Son chooses to reveal him." [10:21-22]

As a response to the successful experiment of using ordinary men in the penetration of the world, a prayer of simple thanksgiving is wholly reasonable, but we need not depend solely upon this, for Matthew's setting is also reasonable. What is important is not the setting, but the jewel that has been preserved! In Matthew's account the section which follows is of especial significance, since it is the famous yoke passage (11:28-30) in which Christ makes His call to commitment, beginning "Come to me."

For our present purposes it is best to concentrate upon the brief prayer itself. What is hard to miss, at the outset, is the naturalness of the prayer and, above all, the sense of intimacy which it reveals. There is no pious wind-up, but the simple "I thank thee, Father." It is not even felt necessary, on this particular occasion, to add adjectives. If God is "Father," that is sufficient. Bishop Cushman tells us how this aspect of Christ's first recorded prayer has struck him. "There is no 'let us pray' preliminary! Jesus just seems to burst forth in prayer to his Father. So real and simple is this conversation between the Son and the Father that one hardly knows where the prayer ends and conversation with the Seventy begins."[2]

It is a matter of intellectual honesty not to claim that Christ introduced to the world, for the first time, the application of

[2] *The Prayers of Jesus, op. cit.*, p. 98.

the term "Father" to Almighty God. Reference to Jewish parallels makes us aware that calling God "Father" was not unique, but, with Christ and His followers, the practice became so prominent that the contrast with anything which came earlier is very great indeed. For practical purposes, therefore, this has come to be a distinct Christian usage. One begins to understand how intense the new emphasis on God as Father really was, when one counts the references to the Father in the Fourth Gospel and finds that there are more than one hundred distinct uses of the word.

Everyone who thinks at all recognizes the fact that calling God "Father" involves the use of a figure of speech, and that the concept has consequent limitations. We could not think at all without figures of speech, because this is one of the chief ways in which we establish *connections*, and connections are necessary for reflection. The completely isolated fact means nothing at all. But, though figures are necessary, they are always deceptive when pressed too far. The ordinary figure normally stresses just one point of similarity and becomes ridiculous, accordingly, when extended to other and irrelevant details. Thus Christ's assertion that He came to cast fire upon the earth is wonderfully clarifying, when we see that He is referring to a fellowship which grows from person to person, as one loving heart sets another on fire, but it would be preposterous for some prosy individual to press the figure in order to make it include destruction. No parable goes on all fours or is intended so to go.

With this warning in mind, we may approach the greatest of all figures of speech, "Father." It does not mean, of course, that there is also a Mother, or that we are begotten as human babies are begotten. It means just one thing: that the Creator and Sustainer of the Universe is at least as solicitous for our welfare as a good parent is for that of a child, even when the child is undeserving. God may be vastly more than this, and undoubtedly is more than we can ask or think, but the basic conviction of Christ, as shown by the opening of His prayer, is that God is at least that much. The best mark, even of an earthly father, is not that he is strong or resourceful or creative, but that he *cares*. It follows that, though he may be just, he is never vindictive, and that, though he may be firm, he is never hateful. His great concern is never for his own prestige or power, but always for the welfare of those for whom he cares. What Christ seems to have felt, more strongly than anything else, was that "the God who is," is at least like such a parent. The conviction is that He cannot be less!

That Christ, in this brief prayer, should address God as Father is significant, but not surprising. What is surprising is the way in which He brings together, in a single context, two aspects of the divine nature which have often seemed to be sharply contrasted or even mutually incompatible. As soon as He has addressed God as Father, He immediately goes on to address Him as "Lord of heaven and earth." The two aspects represent totally different moods. The one is intimate, close, affectionate, but the other involves awe and wonder. Many people think of God in both of these ways, yet in separation from each other. Sometimes we think of God as the One who knows us intimately, by whom even the hairs of our heads are numbered, and who notes tenderly even the sparrow's fall. At other times we think of the Source of the majestic universe as cold, distant, unaffected by desire, the One who set the stars in their courses. The first mood is that of closeness; the second is that of remoteness. In Christ's prayer, the glorious fact is that the two are brought together and held together.

Most of us today are conscious of the fact that the physical universe is almost inconceivably large, and the mere contemplation of the interstellar distances is intrinsically awesome. We quote, approvingly, the words of Pascal, appropriate now, though written more than three hundred years ago: "The eternal silence of these infinite spaces terrifies me." We are well acquainted with the mood which is called "astronomical intimidation," but we sometimes seem to forget that this is not new. It was vivid, not only for Pascal and his friends of the seventeenth century, but for the ancients as well. The first of the writing prophets of Israel evidently felt it, for he wrote, "Seek him that maketh the seven stars and Orion" (Amos 5:8, AV). The ancients, either in Israel or in Greece, did not speak in terms of light years, as we do, but they knew very well that the world was unimaginably large, and once that is known, the addition of a few millions or billions makes little emotional difference.

The opening words of Christ's deeply personal prayer, then, constitute an entire theology. The central conviction is not merely that there is in the universe, in addition to finite creatures, One who cares; nor is it merely that there is a basic Source of the majestic order of the physical universe which makes science, including the science of astronomy, possible; *the central conviction is that the same Being has both of these characteristics.* It is easy to conceive love without power, while it is likewise easy to conceive power without love; what is overwhelming is the union of power and love. What Christ teaches, by the example of His prayer, is that these two conceptions are not separated, but are united in actual existence.

Christ believed that there is in the world, in addition to physical beings and laws and finite conscious creatures, One who combines, in His own Being, the basis of the order in the entire universe, however big it is, and complete knowledge of every creature. There are people who cannot believe this; the concept seems too difficult. How could God, who made the sidereal universe, also care for a poor laborer in Tokyo or in Berlin or in Cairo? This may, indeed, be hard for us to understand, but the probability is that it is hard primarily because of our finitude. We have it on the authority of Christ that God is both Father of our spirits and Lord of heaven and earth, and for many of us that is the place to begin. After all, we have to begin somewhere! The Christian is one who begins with Christ. We accept the stupendous truth because He believed it and made it the basis of His praying.

The kind of religion which comes from the frank acceptance of the central paradox of God's Being is intensely practical. Thus a physical scientist, forcing himself to be absolutely rigorous in not going beyond the evidence, can come to a conclusion about the age of the earth and believe that if the history of the earth is compared to a big book, human history occupies but a few pages. Yet this same man, as he goes to his bed at night, can pray for forgiveness and guidance like a little child. He can do this because there is no incompatibility at all between being an honest researcher and being a follower of Christ, who said, "Whoever does not receive the kingdom of God like a child shall not enter it" (Mark 10:15). The good astronomer is concerned not only with what is revealed at the big end of the telescope, but also with what exists at the small end, and, if he tries to be a Christian, he realizes that God cares about both.

All that is implied in Christ's use of "Father" in His prayer is made specific when He tells about the marvelous inclusiveness of the Father's care. It includes the brute creation, but it includes ourselves in a more specific sense, for we are capable of response. "Are not sparrows two a penny? Yet without your Father's leave not one of them can fall to the ground. As for you, even the hairs of your head have all been counted. So have no fear; you are worth more than any number of sparrows" (Matt. 10:29-31, NEB). Everyone with any experience of life is aware of the fact that this basic conception involves difficulties of an intellectual nature, and the Christian is bound, sooner or later, to face the problem of evil,[3] but it suffices at this point to start where Jesus started. Then we can face problems as we come to them. If we do not accept Christ's starting point, the problem of evil does not arise, *but that is worse!*

The modern world has been greatly indebted to the renowned Jewish philosopher, Martin Buber, for his introduc-

[3] For my own attempt to face it see *The Philosophy of Religion* (New York: Harper & Row, 1957), chap. XVII.

tion into current speech of the phrase "I and thou." His revolutionary insight has been the recognition that any "I-thou" relationship differs, not in degree, but in kind, from any "I-it" relationship. We can *use* an "it" without any sense of moral failure, but, provided we understand, we cannot use a "thou." The "I-thou" relationship, we have come to realize, is the closest and most significant relationship in the whole realm of existence.

Part of the glory of the short prayer of Jesus which appears in Matthew 11:25-26 and Luke 10:21-22 is that Christ addresses God by using the singular form of the pronoun of the second person. He says "I thank *thee*." Here we are at a tremendous distance from the impersonal or even from the familiar *third* person. The point to stress is that Christ's relationship to the Father is immediate and direct. We may use the third person to refer to one who is absent, whom we talk *about*, but we cannot reasonably use the second person except in addressing someone directly. Just as the personal differs in kind from the impersonal, the second person differs in kind from the third.

Even devout and steady readers sometimes miss the shift from the third person to the second in the best loved of all of the Psalms, the 23rd. The Shepherd Psalm begins by repeated reference to God as "he," so that we expect this practice to continue throughout the Psalm. We are grateful for such an expression as "He restoreth my soul," but we are more grateful still when the radical shift occurs. In the depths of the Psalm, even the reference to God as "he" is no longer adequate, for we move over to a direct confrontation. "Yea, though I walk through the valley of the shadow of death, I will fear no evil: for *thou* art with me; *thy* rod and *thy* staff they comfort me. *Thou* preparest a table before me in the presence of mine enemies." There are no greater words in the entire vocabulary of firsthand religion than these modest pronouns: thou, thy, and thee.

When Christ prayed "I thank *thee*," He was asserting the

noblest of traditions, the tradition that the heart of religious experience is not a speculation about God, nor the reflection of what others may say, but direct confrontation. What is basic is the divine encounter, and it is such an encounter which Christ's prayer reveals. It is in this that we should try most to follow Him. It must be said that in trying to follow Him, it is not important whether we use the now largely antique singular form or the generally adopted plural form "you." Some consciously adopt the plural form and call God "you," because they are convinced that such language brings religious expression closer to common life. Others, following the *Book of Common Prayer*, keep to the singular. For more than two hundred years, Quakers sought to retain the singular, not only in prayer, but also in ordinary human conversation. This struggle has now been largely abandoned as not only hopeless, but even harmful, because it tends to set up barriers between persons. The main thing to remember is not whether we use the singular "thou" or the plural "you," but whether we do truly employ the second person. Only when we do this in spirit, regardless of language, do we see prayer for what it most deeply is. The employment of the second person is one way of making sure that prayer is not a disguised public speech, primarily addressed to the listening human audience. All prayer, if it is in conscious conformity to the practice of Christ Himself, is addressed to only one Person, the Lord God Almighty. If humans desire to listen, that may do no harm, but the prayer, when real, is never addressed to them.

Dean Coburn is writing in harmony with Christ's own recorded practice when he tells those who are troubled about prayer how to begin. "The way to begin is to say at this moment, 'O God, *you*. . . .' Once you have said 'God, *you*' and not 'God, *he*' you have begun to pray. This is your response to God."[4]

Because of a surprising combination of intellectual currents, the conception of God as a Person is again under attack, not

[4] *Prayer and Personal Religion, op. cit.,* p. 15.

only among the positivists, which is to be expected, but among leaders in theological seminaries, which is not expected. With all our modernity, there has been a kind of throwback to nineteenth-century thought patterns, so that, among some, it is the mark of a theological and philosophical fad to refuse to speak of God in fully personal terms. The current formula, to which even a bishop of the Church of England has given his support, is to the effect that God may be personal in some vague sense, but is not "a Person." The seriousness of this is that it tends to undermine the possibility of genuine prayer.

Since the drift toward impersonalism has been represented in many quarters, and has even come to be looked upon, by some, as the prime mark of theological sophistication, it needs to be understood and examined. Part of the motivation is the exceedingly elementary one of trying to avoid a naïve or child-like faith in an anthropomorphic God. But it seems odd that this would be considered necessary for contemporary men. The ordinary Christian of our generation, who addresses God as Father, is *not* guilty of a crude anthropomorphism. He recognizes that God is vastly more than a human person, but that if our world is to make sense at all, He is not *less*. If He is not less, then it follows that He is fully personal in the sense that He knows, that He is conscious of finite persons, that He has purposes, and that He cares. This does not imply a body, and it does not entail any of the limitations of our finitude, but it does rest squarely upon the philosophic principle of Sufficient Reason. It holds that it is unreasonable for the creature to be able to demonstrate powers of consciousness which the Creator is unable to enjoy. It is against the ultimate absurdity of this logical consequence that the normal believer in God as Person is rebelling.

The only understandable reason which is given by those who, though devout believers, refuse to speak of God in fully personal terms is their fear that existence involves limitation.[5]

[5] The usual assertion is that existence is a term which may be applicable to things and to finite persons, but cannot be applicable to the Eternal. Therefore there are some, in various denominations, who think it a mark of advancement

Of course it does, but there is nothing wrong with that. Plato went so deeply into this question in his later dialogues that the problem is not a new one for students of philosophy. Anything real involves a limit, in that it is distinct from the unreal. All affirmatives involve negations. If God is fully personal, then He is *not* merely a thing, nor an abstraction. The real alternative to the faith in God in fully personal terms, if it is faith at all, is pantheism, and the intellectual difficulties of pantheism are tremendous. For one thing the pantheist, who thinks that God is everything, cannot have a rational doctrine of sin as something separate from God.

The strangest feature of the impersonalism which has lately been so prominent is its confusion. To say that God is personal, but not a Person, is really double talk. What, in all reason, *can* be personal except a person? Certainly an abstraction cannot be personal, for an abstraction cannot think or love or be wounded. The most damaging aspect of this new theology is therefore its confusion. Many of the upholders, including Bishop Robinson, are men of prayer, and they even say good things about prayer, but, in consistency, they have no Person to whom to pray. How can you pray to a "Ground of Being"? Not at all, if you mean by prayer what Christ evidently meant. Christian prayer is addressed to One who is undoubtedly a Person because we can, without dishonesty, refer to *Him* and, in the direct encounter with Him, can say *"Thou."* Whatever support the upholders of quasi-impersonalism can muster, they cannot appeal to the experience of Jesus Christ in their defense. If they are right, He was wrong! His witness is clear, and it is especially clear in the prayer we are considering now.

---

to refuse to speak of The Existence of God. However laudable this motive is, the practice is certainly confused. The opposite of existence is nonexistence, and there are many, in our generation, who sincerely believe that God is nonexistent, in the sense that He is merely a projection of our wishes. They believe that there is, in fact, no objective referent to what is subjectively imagined. Because this is the urgent question, we can be grateful for some philosophers, particularly the eminent Roman Catholic thinker, Jacques Maritain, who have challenged the entire rejection of existence as applicable to God.

It is not hard to see why many people, and particularly people who are overimpressed with natural science, should have thought that they had to give up the idea of God as personal. They are so deeply impressed with the *impersonality* of the physical universe that they come to the conclusion that God, if He exists at all, is more like a superequation or a formula than like a person. What does the law of gases care about the frail persons who are destroyed by an explosion? A common conclusion is that there is basic to the universe a Supreme Intelligence, but not a person. A good illustration is provided by the late Thomas A. Edison, who said, "A personal God means absolutely nothing to me. . . . I don't believe in the God of the theologians, but that there is a Supreme Intelligence I do not doubt." What he meant, but did not say, was that he did not believe in the God of Jesus Christ.

But how, we reasonably ask, could there be Supreme Intelligence without One who *is* intelligent? Thought without a thinker is nothing at all, just as love is nothing without a lover. People who would reject abstractions in every other realm often seem entirely willing to accept abstractions in the realm of the divine. This is precisely why the study of Christ's prayers is so refreshing, and consequently so corrective of our fads. He clearly understood His heavenly Father to be One who knew Him, and One whom He could know. In short, if His prayers are to be taken as evidence, He was acquainted, by immediate personal experience, not with some supreme mathematical formula, but with One who, in Himself, is the conscious Source of all true formulas and, at the same time, the Lover of individual men and women.

The main intellectual heritage of the Christian faith is both objective and personal. Seldom has this major heritage been more clearly stated, or more brilliantly argued, than it was by Archbishop Temple, especially in his Gifford Lectures, *Nature, Man and God*. According to this heritage of faith and thought, God truly and objectively exists, and is not mere idea. God is completely personal, while we poor mortals are only partially personal. Archbishop Temple returned again and again to the conviction that intelligent purpose provides the only satisfactory explanation of anything. But only a person can exhibit or appreciate intelligent purpose. "Faith in God," wrote Temple, "is precisely the hypothesis that this one principle which is capable of offering a final explanation does in fact explain the universe."[6]

It is in prayer that the logical necessity of envisaging God as "Person" becomes most evident. However grateful we may be for Plato's magnificent concept of "The Good" as developed at the heart of *The Republic*, we know, as Plato himself realized, that The Good is not something to which, or to whom, men can pray. Even the contemporary theologians who refuse to speak of God as Person are better, in this regard, in their practice than in their theory. Professor Paul Tillich has preached a moving sermon on Thanksgiving, but neither he nor anyone else can express thanks to an abstraction. Here we are helped by Dr. Buttrick's fine sentence, "We can hold no comradeship with an abstract noun."[7]

In his brief but penetrating study of the "Our Father," Ernest Fremont Tittle gave a convincing answer to all who fear that in following Christ's practice, they are in danger of anthropomorphism. "We are not trying to say," wrote Tittle, "that the Mind of God is as the mind of a man. We are trying to say that the universal frame is not without a mind. We are not trying to say that the consciousness of God is as the consciousness of a human being. We are trying to say that the universe is not a blind, unconscious force."[8] The being of God is not limited as our being is, but *being in general is no being at all*. Being, in order to be real, must always be definite, and therefore, in one sense, particular.

It is refreshing to find some able leaders of the Christian

[6] *Christian Faith and Life, op. cit.,* pp. 13-14.

[7] *Prayer, op. cit.,* p. 59.

[8] Ernest Fremont Tittle, *The Prayer That Helps Us Live* (New York: The Methodist Book Concern, 1931), p. 9.

movement who are not in the least intimidated by the current impersonalism and who have the courage to announce their faith in God as "a Person." One such is John B. Coburn, whom we have already mentioned. Dean Coburn's refreshing forthrightness and consequent clarity are well demonstrated in the following short paragraph:

God is a Person. He is infinitely more than this, but he is at least this. And this is the place to begin, for if you think of God primarily as a person, then when you speak to him you can say, "You," and "I." When he addresses you, he in turn speaks to a person and also says, "you." Thus a two-way personal conversation, set in a personal relationship, can be set up. This personal conversation is the essence of prayer.[9]

If God were mere goodness or mere intelligence, He would not act, but God, according to the Bible, is One who acts, as well as One who thinks. Above all, He is One who cares. The great conviction is that He made us *because* He cares and is consequently unwilling to deny to us the boon of existence. If Jesus was right, God loves each one of us as though each were the only person in the world! Men and women are not, therefore, mere segments of the faceless crowd, but individuals, each of whom is precious in the Father's eyes. There are honest people who cannot believe this, because they think it is too good to be true. We must respect their honesty, but there is little doubt that in refusing such a faith, they are deliberately separating themselves from the faith of Christ. The Father to whom Christ prayed was such that He could say, "It is not the will of my Father who is in heaven that one of these little ones should perish" (Matt. 18:14).

It is because God is personal that Christ can be His revelation. Being personal, i.e., One who cares, God could not be fully revealed in the starry heavens and, in fact, is not fully revealed there. However moved we may be by the sight of the constellations, we are always aware, as Pascal saw so clearly, that, while we know them, they do not know us. John Baillie,

[9] *Op. cit.*, pp. 12-13.

whose youthful struggle for an honest faith was peculiarly intense, tells how he walked home one frosty midnight, after sharing in a discussion on the existence of God, and stopped to gaze at the starry sky, with the result that his questions were not thereby answered. "Into these deep immensities I hurled my despairing question, but it seemed like nothing and no answer came back."[10]

The astounding and truly revolutionary idea is that if God is personal, His adequate revelation cannot come in anything at all, except a person. This is what Jesus claimed was occurring when He said that no one could know the Father except the son, and that no one could know the Son except the Father. If all of the New Testament were destroyed except Matthew 11:25-27, much of the gospel could be reconstructed from this fragment, as paleontologists reconstruct the character of entire organisms on the basis of a single bone. The gospel is that God is a Person, that each of us is the object of His care, that He can be fully revealed only in a person, and that this revelation has actually occurred in the person of Christ.

Such a faith is in one sense childlike, and that, says Jesus, is in its favor. There are people who are afraid of clarity, because they fear that it may not seem profound. For this reason, deliberate confusion may easily become a cult. But the witness of Christ is all on the other side. He understood the temptation of those who want to appear sophisticated, and He saw that this temptation is as serious in theology as it is in any other realm of thought. Here is where the words of men like the famous Baillie brothers of Scotland are so extremely helpful. These men, John and Donald, were very learned men, each of them sincerely esteeming the other better than himself. Both occupied distinguished chairs, especially at Edinburgh and St. Andrews, but both ended their lives in the faith with which they began in the Free Church Manse of Gairloch. This is nowhere more clearly demonstrated than in the lucid ser-

[10] John Baillie, *The Idea of Revelation in Recent Thought* (London: Oxford University Press, 1956), p. 138.

mons of John Baillie that were published after his death. The last of these sermons, called "When I Awake," is something to which we can turn when we want to see what is meant by Christ's saying that these things, while hidden from the wise and understanding, are revealed unto babes. Speaking of the life to come, into which this beloved man has now entered, he said:

Not even the most learned philosopher or theologian knows what it is going to be like. But there is one thing which the simplest Christian knows—he knows it is going to be all right. Somewhere, some-when, somehow we who are worshipping God here will wake up to see Him as He is, and face to face; but where or when we know not, or even whether it will be in a "where" and a "when," that is, in space and time at all. No doubt it will be utterly different from anything we have ever imagined or thought about it. No doubt God Himself will be unimaginably different from our present conception of Him. But He will be unimaginably different only because He will be unimaginably better. The only thing we do certainly know is that our highest hopes will be more than fulfilled, and our deepest longings more than gratified."[11]

A significant remaining point to be made about the first recorded prayer of Christ is that its mood is the mood of thanks. Thanksgiving is the most generous and gracious element in prayer and has always been important when the followers of Christ have stayed close to His example. For instance, it is suggested by Colossians 3:14-17 that thanks was the dominant feature of early Christian gatherings. Thankfulness is mentioned three times in this one short passage. Indeed, worship *is* thanks!

In a famous passage of *A Serious Call*, William Law has taught us how purifying gratitude is. Here is the paragraph:

If anyone would tell you the shortest, surest way to all happiness and all perfection, he must tell you to make a rule to yourself to thank and praise God for everything that happens to you. It is certain that whatever seeming calamity happens to you, if you

[11] *Christian Devotion, op. cit.,* p. 113.

thank and praise God for it you turn it into a blessing. If you could work miracles, therefore, you could not do more for yourself than by this thankful spirit. It heals and turns all that it touches into happiness.[12]

A good rule of prayer is found in following our Lord's example and beginning with thanks, thus making every day a day of thanksgiving. If we pay attention to the story of the raising of Lazarus, we see how Christ began with thanks, even in an agonizing situation. "And Jesus lifted up his eyes and said, 'Father, I thank thee that thou hast heard me'" (John 11:41). Thanksgiving involves so much more than it appears to involve. Even the prayer of adoration, says Dean Coburn, "is to thank God for God!" while the prayer of thanksgiving is "to thank Him for what He does." And then this same scholar tells why the attitude of thanks is so healing. "Your attention then is directed away from yourself—your needs, your problems, your sins, and all the rest which is *you*—and outward toward God."[13]

Wonderful as thanks is, honesty compels us to point out that it is not foolproof.[14] It is a significant fact that the one prayer which Christ mentioned as an example of how *not* to pray was a prayer of thanks. The Pharisee was thankful, but he was thankful in the wrong way, and for the wrong things. The Parable of the Pharisee and the Publican, which is undoubtedly a parable concerned with prayer, presents the Pharisee as thankful while all that the tax collector can pray is "God be merciful to me a sinner." The Pharisee's prayer was "God, I thank thee that I am not like other men, extortioners, unjust, adulterers, or even like this tax collector. I fast twice a week, I give tithes of all that I get" (Luke 18:11-12).

Thanks is primary, then, but thanks must not be so couched

[12] *Op. cit.*, p. 101.
[13] *Op. cit.*, p. 34.
[14] Perhaps no good thing is foolproof. Charity is glorious, and we are commanded to give, but the hard truth is that the giver may develop a sense of superiority to the recipient. Penitence is wonderful, and certainly it is necessary, but the penitent runs the risk of becoming self-righteous in his humility.

as to call attention to ourselves. Our thanksgiving must never become a subtle form of boasting. The secret lies in making the emphasis on what God has done, rather than upon what we have been able to accomplish. The dangers of thanksgiving are great, but the dangers of trying to pray without it are greater.

❧ ❧

CHAPTER VI

Prayers Before the Cross

"Father, the hour has come."
John 17:1

THERE IS NO DOUBT that the most loved of Christ's recorded prayers are those which He uttered immediately prior to the tragic hours of trial and crucifixion. This is especially true of His prayer for the Church, which occupies the whole of the seventeenth chapter of John, and which has sometimes been termed the High Priestly Prayer. At least three contempory devotional writers have given careful attention to this, which is far the longest of the prayers reported to have been uttered by our Lord. Leonard Griffith, minister of London's City Temple, devotes four chapters to this prayer in his *The Eternal Legacy from the Upper Room*, Bishop Ralph S. Cushman devotes more than half of his book, *The Prayers of Jesus*, to this one prayer, and James G.S.S. Thomson, in *The Praying Christ*, makes the seventeenth chapter of John the subject of an entire chapter of exposition.

The one long prayer attributed to Jesus appears in John as part of what we know as the Farewell Discourses, which are collected in Chapters 14, 15, 16, and 17. Anyone who seeks to make a scholarly approach to this material is soon convinced that the author of the Fourth Gospel is, in this section, concerned more with the sayings than with the historical order in which these sayings occurred. It is not even clear where the major discourses were given, and perhaps it is not important that we should know. That not all of the discourses were given in the famous Upper Room, where Jesus ate the Last Supper with the Twelve, and where he washed their feet, is indicated by the fact that He said, "Rise, let us go hence" (14:31).

Christians have come to treasure the collection of sayings in these four tightly packed chapters and to turn to them for devotional purposes. It is in this collection that we find such gems as "In my Father's house are many rooms," "Let not your hearts be troubled, neither let them be afraid," "I am the true vine and my Father is the vinedresser," and, above all, "This is my commandment, that you love one another as I have loved you." For those interested in Christ's doctrine and practice of prayer, the section is important, not only because it includes His longest spoken prayer, but also because of the repetition of a promise which is startling in its lack of qualifications. At one point (15:16) He is reported as saying that "whatever you ask the Father in my name, he may give it to you." A promise so unqualified has often been extremely comforting, but we must beware of interpreting this too simply, for Christ Himself said, in another connection, "if it be possible."

It is very important that we face honestly the paradox suggested by the fact that not all prayers, and not even all of Christ's own prayers, have been answered simply and directly. There is, for example, a sense in which Christ's prayer for the unity of His Church has not been answered affirmatively during all the succeeding centuries of conflict and strain. Peter was disloyal even after Christ prayed for him. Many people isolate one side of Christ's message and assume that if they pray hard enough, they will get what they want. And, it must be said, there are statements which, taken alone, seem to say this. To the father of a stricken boy Christ said, "All things are possible to him who believes" (Mark 9:23). Expectation seems to gain support from the confident statement concerning the brief parable of the mustard seed. "For truly, I say to you, if you have faith as a grain of mustard seed, you will say to this mountain, 'Move hence to yonder place,' and it will move; and nothing will be impossible to you" (Matt. 17-20).

The tragedy which occurs in many lives, when such expressions are noted without the balance of other aspects of both the teaching and the example of Christ, is that there is frequently a complete revulsion following failure. Over and over we get the report, "I prayed and nothing happened; the one I loved so much, for whose survival I prayed, was taken from me, as if I had not prayed at all." The people who say this have read the words of Christ, "Therefore I tell you, whatever you ask in prayer, believe that you receive it, and you will" (Mark 11:24), but the fact is that they believe and they do not receive. It is a great help to such persons, and a possible means of avoiding subsequent spiritual disaster, to recognize that such statements, taken out of the context of the whole, are inadequate. There is no better means of providing balance than to concentrate on Christ's own prayers in the last days before He died. It is helpful to remember the teaching of the noted American philosopher, Josiah Royce, to the effect that one-sided propositions can never express the truth adequately. The truth resides in the totality!

It is not necessary to think that the entire prayer of John 17 was uttered all at once and remembered by the Apostles, who presumably were present. Such a long prayer would be very difficult to remember verbatim, whereas the short one which we have studied in Chapter V of this book could be remembered with ease. Since the discourses which precede the long prayer are evidently collections of words said on various subjects, at various times, and united by the author for literary effect, the same may be true of the long prayer. Jesus *could* have uttered the prayer all at the same time, but its power would not be lessened if such were not the case. Even the beginning scholar is likely to note some passages which sound more like preaching than like praying, and which may, in fact, reflect the later experiences of the infant Church after the resurrection had occurred. A prime illustration is that of John 17:3, "And this is eternal life, that they know thee the only true God, and Jesus Christ whom thou hast sent." Here is a doctrine which seems to be more in the mood of the Epistles than of the Gospels. It is odd, for example, for Christ to speak of Himself in the third person. In the context of this prayer the pronoun "me' would be more natural. In any case, the combined expression "Jesus Christ" is a favorite expression of the later Church, found often in Acts and the Epistles, but apparently not normally used during our Lord's earthly life.

Any sensitive person will be bound to approach the prayer of John 17 with reverent wonder. We are hearing, not an argument, and not a lecture about religion, but, instead, we are listening in on the direct communion between Christ and His heavenly Father. In a superlative sense, this belongs not to literature *about* religion, but to the literature *of* religion. It is no wonder that this is one of the most treasured chapters of Scripture. "Reading it," says Leonard Griffith, "is like stepping inside a beautiful and sacred shrine where the atmosphere is holy and hushed, and we have only the instinct to fall to our knees in humble adoration."[1]

The long prayer falls, conveniently, into four major parts. The first part, verses 1-5, is Christ's appeal for Himself in the light of His approaching bodily death. He reflects His keen sense of the importance of time. What has been long expected is now at hand. Already He has emphasized this, before the Last Supper, in a brief prayer, the remembrance of which we owe to John. "Now is my soul troubled. And what shall I say? 'Father, save me from this hour'? No, for this purpose I have come to this hour" (12:27). We shall consider this brief prayer more fully later in the chapter, but it is helpful to note it here, because it stresses the sense of the fullness of time. It stresses *kairos* rather than *chronos*. Some hours are vastly fuller than others and deserve far more attention. It was by a fine

[1] *The Eternal Legacy from the Upper Room* (New York: Harper & Row, 1963), p. 156.

instinct that the authors of all four Gospels gave so much attention to the last few days of Christ on earth. Only in the ending, as in a tragic play, does the meaning of the whole appear.

When, in the brief prayer, we have the sense of destiny "For this purpose I have come to this hour," we have a preview of Christ's memorable words when He appeared before Pilate. When Pilate said, "So you are a king?" Jesus answered, "You say that I am a king. For this I was born, and for this I have come into the world, to bear witness to the truth" (John 18:37). It was this passage, with its sense of manifest destiny, that inspired the late Edith Hamilton to entitle her Life of Christ, *Witness to the Truth*. Timing is important, and when the witness is called to the stand he must go, even though the ordeal is hard. What can help Christ's followers most, in this connection, is the recognition of being under command and therefore not masters of their own time. Christ's prayers express His sense of being under the Father's orders and therefore ready for crisis. The prayers we are considering were His means of *getting ready* for crisis. They were advance testings.

When we meditate on the significance of the hour of testing, "Father, the hour has come," we can see the reason for the wide appreciation of what is perhaps the most successful of contemporary hymns, Fosdick's "God of grace and God of glory." This prayer, written to be sung at the dedication of The Riverside Church, New York, is now used in nearly all denominations, and by Christians of nearly all theological emphases. A good part of the reason is because of the way in which the hymn reflects the prayer of Jesus, in its stress on "this hour" and on "the living of these days." Many will attest that their own determination is strengthened by singing, along with their fellows, "Grant us wisdom, grant us courage, for the facing of this hour." The more familiar we are with John 12:27 and John 17:1, the deeper is the emotion which such phrases engender.

The second part of the long prayer, verses 6-19, is petition that is intercessory. Christ prays here, not for strength for Himself in facing the coming ordeal, but for strength for his immediate followers. These men were very important for the whole world, because, if they should fail, there was no other way of assuring the continuance of the redemptive leaven, without which the world could not rise. Though these, hopefully, would be followed by a host of future witnesses, for the time being the sole responsibility was upon them. For the moment, for this crucial "hour," they were the saving salt, but what if they should fail? What if the saltness would be lost? It would then be worth absolutely nothing.

It is no wonder, then, that Christ felt impelled to pray for His closest associates in the sacred cause. His prayer constitutes a re-emphasis of the idea that the way of a redemptive society is the only possible way. For the moment, He did not pray for the world, but for the little band who were so important *to* the world. If they were the light of the world, the best way to help the world was to help them.

The paradox of Christian worldliness is deeply embedded in this part of the prayer. There is a sense in which the little band is not of the world. This is because it has been given standards which are in contrast to all worldly standards. The idea had already been made vivid by the acted parable of washing the feet of His followers, thus rejecting utterly the worldly ideal of prestige and status. It had been expressed earlier, according to the Synoptic Gospels, in words, but the foot washing, stressed by John, indicated the need of something more than words. Christ had already said to the Twelve, "If any one would be first, he must be last of all and servant of all" (Mark 9:35) and, even more vividly, as all of the Synoptics attest, "You know that those who are supposed to rule over the Gentiles lord it over them, and their great men exercise authority over them. But it shall not be so among you" (Mark 10:42-43). Here "Gentiles" signify the world and worldly ways. Because Christ was inaugurating a potential revolution in values, the little band, it could be truly said, were "not of the world," though the sequel showed that in fact they often re-flected the values of the world with alarming accuracy.

Christians, the great prayer indicates, while ideally not *of* the world, are emphatically *in* the world. Here the prayer brings to a climax the theme of penetration to which the metaphors of salt, light, and leaven evidently refer. As the Father has sent the Son to penetrate the world, so, in turn, the Son sends His Apostles. The location of the Church is not in some place separate from common life, but *in the world!*

In the third part of the long prayer is Christ's intercession for later generations of His apostolate, i.e., the Church. Since some of us try to be part of this group, we have every right to conclude that Christ was praying for us. By means of the chain reaction, through which the word of one would reach another, there would soon be participants of the cause who stood at several removes, both temporally and spatially, from the primitive fellowship.

One of the major petitions regarding future and remote followers was a prayer for their unity. The degree to which this part of the prayer has influenced the entire ecumenical move-ment in our century is beyond calculation, but we know it is very great. The key petition in this connection is "that they may become perfectly one, so that the world may know that thou hast sent me and hast loved them even as thou hast loved me" (John 17:23).

It is obvious that unity is difficult even in a small company like that of the Twelve, who were in fact far from united. How much more difficult is it among millions of people scattered all over the earth, reflecting the inevitable growth of particular traditions! What is important to know is that unity is some-thing to be *achieved*, and that, like freedom, it can come only at the end of an arduous process and never at the beginning. This is vividly expressed in Ephesians 4:13, in the translation of *The New English Bible*, by "So shall we all at last attain to the unity inherent in our faith."

Sometimes contemporary Christians, as they consider

Christ's prayer for unity, are ashamed of the fact that they belong to denominations, but this is almost certainly a mistake. Though denominations, as we know them, have been part of the Christian scene for only a little more than three hundred years, and may well be a passing phenomenon, there is no doubt that they have contributed much to the richness of the world-wide Christian Cause. For the most part, each denomination has contributed something which otherwise might have been forgotten, or might never have been adequately understood. Personally, I am grateful for the way in which the Brethren have maintained and glorified the practice of foot washing, for the way in which Friends have developed, for all to copy if they will, the moving experience of group silence, for the way in which Roman Catholics have developed various *orders* for both men and women, and so on with many more.

What we need in the effort to achieve the unity for which Christ prayed, is not a dull uniformity, but a variety with mutual appreciation. How wonderful if each group, when it makes some discovery, could feel that it holds this discovery in trust for the entire Church and should give every encouragement to others to imitate it. The paradox is that a faithful Christian society nourishes something that is unique, only in the hope that it will no longer be unique. This leads to the still deeper paradox that we cannot save our lives except by losing them. The only way to be loyal to a particular heritage is to share it and thus to make it universal.

In preparation for the World Council of Churches in Amsterdam, in August, 1948, those who planned the public worship arrived at a brilliant decision. They undertook to provide public worship each day, for all, in as many authentic ways as were feasible. Instead of deciding, as they might reasonably have been expected to do, to plan an eclectic service to be repeated each day, they decided to ask each major group to conduct worship in its own best tradition, with all others invited as attenders and participators. Thus there was, one day, a Lutheran service, once an Anglican morning prayer, once a

Quaker meeting, once a Calvinist service, and so on. The resulting effect was almost overwhelming, and was obviously greater
than could have been the effect of a compromise solution of
the problem. What all then realized was that there is a finer
unity in the richness of a patchwork quilt than there is in one
monotonous dull gray, which offends nobody, but also inspires
nobody.

The unity we seek as we try to provide answers to Christ's
prayer for unity in the future Church, is one which is compatible with difference. This is, in fact, what is coming to pass
in many places, and is something about which we can reasonably rejoice. We do not have a single monolithic Church, but
there is emerging something that may be far better—the recognition that there are many rooms in the Father's house. While
the rooms are different, the roof is the same, for it covers all.
However big the Church of Jesus Christ may be, it is at least
bigger than my church, and there are many now who say the
same about their own. We are not so rich in resources that we
can afford to neglect any that are genuine. There is one
Protestant retreat house which has, on the wall, an etching of
Cardinal Newman, and why not? Newman has something to
say to all, just as John Woolman has something to say to
all. A Roman Catholic retreat house, if it knows what it
is about, will make available *John Woolman's Journal* along
with other devotional classics. It was in this mood that after
the death of Donald Baillie, Hugh Montefiore wrote about him
that "he was not just a Presbyterian Divine; like all the saints
he belongs to the whole Church of God."

The final part of the prayer for the Church is very brief,
being a petition for something more important than unity,
viz., love. "I made known to them thy name, and I will make
it known, that the love with which thou hast loved me may
be in them, and I in them" (John 17:26). This is the end!
"From this prayer," writes the minister of the City Temple,
following the chronology of John, "he went straight out to the
betrayal, the trial, the scourging and the Cross. He did not

speak to his disciples again. It is a wonderful and precious
thing to remember that, before those terrible hours, his last
words were not of defeat and despair but of triumph and
glory."[2]

According to John, Jesus went, after praying the prayer for
the Church, "across the Kidron valley, where there was a garden, which he and his disciples entered" (18:1). Then, immediately, came the betrayal and arrest there. The Synoptic
authors, however, report at this point in the story one of the
most appealing scenes of the entire Gospel, the scene in which
Christ prays in the Garden. What occurred there has taken a
deep hold on the imagination of many generations of Christian
people and constitutes one of our chief evidences of what
Christ's life of prayer really was. It is a fine example of His
resorting to prayer in the face of impending crisis or decision.

Why John does not also include the prayer in the Garden of
Gethsemane we do not know, but it is reasonable to suppose
that he felt that the long prayer, already discussed, was in some
sense a substitute. Furthermore, John had already provided a
brief expression of the same inner struggle which the prayer
in Gethsemane represents. This prayer, and its immediate
sequel, already mentioned earlier in this chapter, is as follows:

"Now is my soul troubled. And what shall I say? 'Father, save
me from this hour'? No, for this purpose I have come to this hour.
Father, glorify thy name." Then a voice came from heaven, "I have
glorified it, and I will glorify it again." [John 12:27-28]

Here is the mood of Gethsemane, with essentially the same
struggle, and with the same victory. The unique feature is the
way in which this short prayer constitutes a true conversation,
including the Father's response. Here was a prayer that was
literally "answered." We are told that the members of the
crowd heard the answer and said it was thunder, while others
said that an angel had spoken to Him. Their conviction was
that He was not speaking into the void, with no response.

[2] *Ibid.*, p. 192.

The theme of anguish, "Now is my soul troubled," is the opening theme in the prayer in the Garden. As on the Mountain of Transfiguration, He left most of the disciples and took the inner circle, Peter, James, and John, to an advanced position. To them, and only to them, did He confide the degree to which He was distressed and troubled. Having revealed to them His agony of spirit, He went on still farther and there prayed alone, falling upon the ground. How the others knew what He prayed well enough to report it, we do not know, but the presumption is that they knew because He told them.

What He prayed, Mark tells us, was again connected with "the facing of this hour," exactly in the mood of John 12:27. He prayed, says Mark (who, if Papias was right, got his information from Peter) that "the hour might pass from him" (14:35). We cannot know what was in His mind, but it is obvious that He did not want to die, and that death appeared to be involved in the crisis of this "hour." Long before, He had asked the sons of Zebedee if they were able to drink the cup that He would drink or be baptized with His baptism (Mark 10:38), and, with these same men near him in Gethsemane, Christ faced realistically the full drinking of the cup which He had foreseen.

The Gethsemane accounts of Matthew and Mark are essentially identical, but only Mark preserves the intimate word "Abba" with which the actual prayer begins. Luke's account is an abbreviation of Mark's, but he adds two important features, the appearance of an angel, strengthening Christ, and the physical details of the agonizing experience. "And being in an agony he prayed more earnestly; and his sweat became like great drops of blood falling down upon the ground" (22:44). Even the casual student is likely to notice the reverberations, in the Garden Prayer, of what we ordinarily call the Lord's Prayer. Luke begins both of these with the simple "Father," and in the Garden Prayer, includes the essence both of "Thy will be done" and "Lead us not into temptation." Luke emphasizes the temptation theme by using it both as a beginning and as an end. His account starts, "And when he came to the place he said to them, 'Pray that you may not enter into temptation,'" and in the end he has Christ repeat the same words to the disciples who have been sleeping during His agony: "Rise and pray that you may not enter into temptation" (22:46). This, therefore, we may remember as one of the chief things for which Christ asks His followers, including ourselves, to pray.

The appropriateness of the double request about temptation is evident, when we contemplate the fact that every life includes constant decisions, and that the temptation to deviate from the best that we know is unending. Our Lord was speaking for every man when He said, "The spirit indeed is willing, but the flesh is weak." Man is a creature of glorious possibilities, but also a creature of repeated failures. In countless cases the failures consist, not in choosing some positive evil, but in deciding for some lesser good. There was a deep sense in which Christ's own experience in the Garden was a renewal of the temptation in the wilderness. As the climax approached, how could He be sure that the whole conception of the suffering Messiah was not a mistake? Nowhere else is the extremely human side of Christ's double nature more truly revealed. Here is One who is, in every respect, "tempted as we are" (Heb. 4:15), yet also One who bows in perfect obedience to the Father's will.

The contrast between Christ's anguish and the sleepiness of the disciples is dramatic. Though Luke tells us of only once that Christ returns from His advanced position of prayer to find them asleep, Mark and Matthew report that He found them sleeping three times. This repetition helps to make vivid the way in which Christ prayed the same words several times, perhaps more discouraged each time, because of the lack of appreciation on the part of even His closest followers of what was occurring. There is a powerful appeal in the fact that His first expression of disappointment was directed to Peter alone: "Simon, are you asleep? Could you not watch one hour?"

(Mark 14:37). Here was the leader of the Apostles, the man who talked a brave fight, yet desire for his own comfort had dominated his action. Peter had greatness in him, a greatness demonstrated both by his original insight into who Jesus was, and later, by his steadfastness following the resurrection; for the moment, however, he was a weak, comfort-loving man. The outlook for the Church was not optimistic if it had to be built on this kind of "rock." Indeed, it was more like rubble than like solid building stone.

The heart of the experience in the Garden of Gethsemane, and the aspect of the story which has appealed to millions, particularly in song, is the victorious struggle of Christ to conform His will to the Father's will. The terrific fact is that even our Lord did not get what He wanted, but accepted something else in victorious submission. The prayer experiences of all subsequent generations have been influenced by the phrase "nevertheless, not as I will, but as thou wilt." Millions have learned that the Father wants us to open up our full hearts to Him, holding nothing back, presenting all our problems as well as all our desires, yet adding sincerely at the end, "if it be thy will."

The more we contemplate, the more we are likely to agree with Dean Coburn that Christ's prayer "Thy will be done" is really the best prayer there is. "He asked God very specifically that the suffering he saw before him the next day be taken away. Suffering was not what *he* wanted. Yet he knew that what *God* wanted would in the long run be best for his work, for the world and for himself. Therefore, he concluded his prayer, 'Thy will be done.' "[3]

If we follow Christ's example and remember to mean, as well as to say, "if it be thy will," any honest prayer is suitable. Some are always telling us that we ought not to pray for personal things or for trifling things. But why not? Not one of us is really as high-minded as that sort of rigid limitation indicates. Certainly we worry about little things, but, as John Baillie

[3] *Prayer and Personal Religion, op. cit.,* p. 46.

said, "If anything is big enough to *worry* about, it is big enough
to *pray* about."[4] There must be no artificial reserve. Of course,
it is true that "your Father knows what you need before you
ask him" (Matt. 6:8), but if we were to be stopped by that,
we should have to give up prayer entirely, and we are quite
sure that Christ's words did not imply this drastic conclusion.
The answer is that, though God knows what we want, *He
wants us to tell Him,* as a human parent wants his child to tell
him. In genuine prayer, it is a mistake to claim to be more
high-minded than we really are. One of the basic rules of
prayer, then, is Don't lie. Dean Coburn puts this point vividly.
"Be yourself," he says. "Do not pretend. It is the only honest,
open way to God. Anyhow, to try to hide anything from God
is a sheer waste of time. He already knows everything that is
in your heart."[5]

The hardest intellectual problem facing many people, who
are unable to accept the reality of prayer, centers on the question of the divine will. In great sincerity many say, "Whatever
is to be is already according to God's will. Why, therefore,
should a poor finite creature pray? Prayer is either blasphemous
or superfluous. If we try to *change* God's will, it is blasphemous;
if we know we cannot change His will, it is superfluous." Because this difficulty is felt by many good people, it is very important that an answer be provided. If we take this difficulty
seriously, the best approach to an answer is to reconsider what
prayer is intended to be. It is not an effort to tell God what to
do, but rather an effort to tell Him what we, as poor living
mortals, need. William Temple dealt with this problem with
characteristic clarity when he wrote:

We are not, in our prayers, trying to suggest to God something
He has not thought of. That would plainly be ridiculous. Nor are
we trying to change His mind. That would be an enterprise blasphemous in the attempt, and calamitous in the accomplishment.[6]

---

[4] *Christian Devotion, op. cit.,* p. 47.
[5] *Op. cit.,* p. 18.
[6] *Christian Faith and Life, op. cit.,* p. 107.

The mistake of the people who say "it is absurd to try to change God's will" is that they are thinking of God in less than personal terms. They are thinking of some unchangeable formula, as cold and bloodless as an equation, and, of course, that cannot be changed. But if God is really the Infinite Person, as Christ implies, there is no good reason for our not being entirely open with Him. The heart of prayer, for Jesus, is the expression of pure trust and utter devotion, a result of overflowing affection. Prayer is conversation with the Father, not an effort to dictate to Him. This is made perfectly clear whenever we add "If it be thy will." We are very glad, in fact, that we cannot dictate, since we should certainly dictate, in many cases, the wrong things entirely. Every humble man who prays is exceedingly glad that not all of his prayers have been answered in the affirmative. "If I thought," says John Baillie, "that God were going to grant me all my prayers simply for the asking, without ever passing them under His own gracious review, without ever bringing to bear upon them His own greater wisdom, I think there would be very few prayers that I should dare to pray."[7]

Here is very great wisdom from the pen of one who writes no more. Real prayer can be both unreserved and humble, unreserved because we present any and all of our needs to the Father, humble because we are well aware that we are not wise enough to know which of our desires ought to be fulfilled. Prayer, as the New Testament teaches, is emphatically not a slick device according to which, when we say the right words, we are sure of the outcome. The promise, fundamentally, is not that the Father always does precisely as we ask, but rather that He always *hears*.

The humility of Christ's prayer strikes us very deeply as we study His words. His humility was compatible with His sorrow. We know of His sorrow because of what He said to the three of the inner circle: "My soul is very sorrowful, even to death" (Mark 14:34). But, even in His sorrow, He realized that it

[7] *Op. cit.*, p. 49.

might be right for the occasion of his sorrow to proceed to its tragic completion. So He did not pray, unconditionally, that the impending climax should be avoided. He "prayed that, *if it were possible*, the hour might pass from him" (Mark 14:35). The outcome, of course, showed that it was not possible, in consistency with the Father's purpose. In this obedient accept-ance of the possible lies the major moral victory. Dante was reflecting this in writing his most famous line, "In His will is our peace."

We have no doubt that the scene in Gethsemane is funda-mental to a Christian understanding of prayer and particularly to the urgent problem of "unanswered prayer." In one sense Christ's prayer in the Garden was not answered, because the cup did not pass without His drinking it to the full, but, in another sense, His prayer was gloriously answered. The prayer was answered in and through His suffering. The cup was not removed, but the drinking of it became redemptive. Herein lies the paradox of negation and ultimate fulfillment.

The end of the story of the prayer in Gethsemane is superbly brief. "Rise, let us be going; see, my betrayer is at hand" (Mark 14:42). Professor Stendahl speaks for many when he writes, "The majestic note is recaptured as Jesus goes to meet His executioners."[8] After this, there came betrayal, arrest, and trials. He must have been praying all of the time, but there is no more record of His prayers until we come to those uttered in the crucifixion itself.

Christians of succeeding generations have rightly lumped to-gether the agony in the Garden and the agony on the cross, finding in the contemplation of the combined spectacle some-thing recurrently humbling and regenerating. We may not struggle until our sweat falls like great drops of blood, but we are better men and women when we face honestly the fact that this occurred in the experience of our Lord. One of our chief means of grace, therefore, is found in periodic reminders of the ancient fact. Those of our generation who feel no emotional re-

[8] *Peake's Commentary, op. cit.,* p. 795.

sponse to the words Gethsemane and Golgotha are not to be envied. We were not there, but we can at least engage in commemoration. How powerful such commemoration can be in the production of contrition and desire for the amendment of life, is magnificently illustrated in one of the preserved prayers of Doctor Samuel Johnson. Written two hundred years ago, it is perfectly timeless, especially in reference to "this awful remembrance."

Almighty God, by whose mercy I am now permitted to commemorate my Redemption by our Lord Jesus Christ; grant that this awful remembrance may strengthen my Faith, enliven my Hope, and encrease my Charity; that I may trust in Thee with my whole heart, and do good according to my power. Grant me the help of thy Holy Spirit, that I may do thy will with diligence, and suffer it with humble patience: so that when Thou shalt call me to Judgement, I may obtain forgiveness and acceptance for the sake of Jesus Christ, our Lord and Saviour. Amen.[9]

[9] *Doctor Johnson's Prayers, op. cit.,* p. 4.

CHAPTER VII

❧ §❧

Prayers on the Cross

"Father, into thy hands I commit my spirit!"
Luke 23:46

THE SPACE ALLOTTED in all of the Gospels to the last days of Christ on earth is very great in proportion to the space devoted to other events. If His life were written with similar detail at all points, the resulting volume would be a large one. For this apparent disproportion we all know the reason. Christ could not have taken hold of the imagination of a great part of the human race merely as a gifted Teacher or even as a miraculous Healer. The effectiveness of the faith which He proclaimed was guaranteed by the way He suffered, by the way He died, and by the way He rose. The most important part of His earthly life was, therefore, its *end*. In saying this, we do not need to minimize His gaiety, His parables, His affection for persons. We can sympathize with Baron von Hügel when he wrote, "I don't like Christians who have concentrated only on the Cross; *Christianity is the whole life of Christ*."[1]

We want to contemplate all of Christ's life, for in the total confrontation lies our hope of renewal, but there is no doubt that the scene on the cross is more moving than is any other. The utterances on the cross, so few and so incisive, have been

[1] Baron Friedrich von Hügel, *Letters to a Niece* (Chicago: Henry Regnery Company, 1957), p. 25.

the theme of many books.[2] In countless communities Good Friday is now recognized annually by three-hour services in which the seven utterances are honored by the spoken word, by song, and by silent meditation. The conscious effort to encourage such remembrance is usually a deepening experience. The consequence is that the seven last words are better known by the general public than are almost any other of Christ's vocal expressions.

We have to use all four of the Gospels in order to count seven utterances from the cross. One comes from both Mark and Matthew, three come from Luke alone, and three come only from John. The late Gaius Glenn Atkins made the happy observation that the seven utterances employ, metaphorically, three different directions of space. Some words, those to His mother and to the beloved disciple (John 19:26-27), were directed *down*, to the foot of the cross; some, the prayers, were directed *up*, to the Father; one, the gracious utterance to the repentant thief (Luke 23:43), was directed *laterally*. The lateral sentence, "Truly, I say to you, today you will be with me in Paradise," though not a prayer, is of momentous significance for the total Gospel. Its significance lies in the fact that it shows that no external rite is necessary for eternal companionship with the Father. It shows, beyond all cavil, that nothing except reality is required, however helpful anything else may be. It is central to Christ's Gospel to know, not only that if we have the reality, nothing is required, but also that if we do not have the reality, nothing else will suffice.

If we concentrate upon the four utterances on the cross, as recorded in the Synoptic Gospels, it is striking to realize that three of these are prayers. That is, all are prayers, with the exception of the statement to the penitent criminal. The fact that so many are prayers tells us something of great importance about the entire crucifixion event. We have noted, in preceding

[2] Two of the most helpful are *From the Cross: The Seven Last Words*, by Gaius Glenn Atkins (New York: Harper & Row, 1937), and *Daily Meditations on the Seven Last Words*, by G. Ernest Thomas (Nashville: Abingdon Press, 1959).

pages, many evidences of the importance of prayer in Christ's life, but prayer became an even more dominant feature in the final tragic hours. In fact, prayer was His only recourse. The Apostles, on whom He might have depended for campassionate fellowship, were mostly absent, and the support of the crowd was dissipated. Those who had heard Him gladly, listening so attentively that the religious leaders were fearful of a general uprising in His favor, now joined in the jeers and derision. Anyone who knows anything of the cowardice of a mob is deeply moved when he reads, "And those who passed by derided him, wagging their heads, and saying, 'Aha! You who would destroy the temple and build it in three days, save yourself, and come down from the cross!'" (Mark 15:29-30.).

There were many, we are told, who taunted Him and challenged Him to work a miracle in His own behalf. This shows how widely His reputation as a performer of miraculous acts, particularly in connection with healing, had been popularly recognized. Not only the passers-by, but also the rulers, the soldiers, and even one of the two criminals flung the taunt. One of the criminals said, "Are you not the Christ? Save yourself and us!" (Luke 23:39). Christ had tried desperately to provide a different conception of what the Messiahship meant, explaining patiently that it involved suffering rather than pomp and pride, but it is clear that most people, including the Twelve, did not really grasp the revolutionary significance of what He had said.

Instead of making a spectacle of relief, which presumably He might have done, Jesus *prayed*. And He did not pray for a miraculous escape, as some of the people evidently expected. In short, He was true to the decision made when He was tempted in the wilderness. In the multiple temptation, concerning bread, power, and notoriety, Christ had been reminded of the words of the 91st Psalm, "He will give his angels charge of you to guard you." Could He not, then, be miraculously saved, even if He deliberately jumped from a high pinnacle? Yet all this had been resolutely rejected as unworthy, provided the idea of the suffering servant were to be given embodiment. That battle having been won once and for all, the taunts of the various onlookers at the crucifixion affected Him not at all.

Christ, we must remember, was not the only person who has ever been crucified. Many slaves suffered this ignominy and pain under the rule of Rome, and two convicted criminals were executed in this way on the same day that Christ died. Even more horrible torture, leading to death, has been suffered by men in our century. The uniqueness, then, lay not in the mere fact of crucifixion, but in the totality of the experience, with the rejection of miracle and the practice of prayer appearing as crucial elements. Baron von Hügel stated the issue pointedly. "Religion is not based on miracles," he wrote. "Put them on one side. They are often symbolical; at any rate the supernatural life is not based on them. The supernatural life is the life of prayer."[3] If prayer is the essence of the supernatural life, Christ's prayers on the cross are wholly in character. His call was to reveal the Father, and the climax of this revelation came as the One, who could have saved Himself, turned instead to the kind of prayer which ended in victory.

There is no better point of view from which to see the entire scene of the crucifixion than from that of the Roman military officer who was in charge of the multiple execution. All three of the Synoptics mention this unnamed centurion. Because he was free from the emotional bias of the local religious leaders, or even from that of the populace, he could view the scene objectively, and it seems to have convinced him of the validity of Christ's claim. He pronounced his own verdict. Luke says this verdict was "Certainly this man was innocent!" (23:47), but Mark, with Matthew following him, goes further and reports the Roman officer as declaring, "Truly this man was the Son of God!" (15:39). This is the beginning of the long story of the evangelizing effect of the crucifixion. Even Mahatma Gandhi, never officially Christian, was so deeply moved by the entire crucifixion record that at his famous prayer meetings

[3] Von Hügel, *op. cit.*, pp. 31-32.

in India, one of the favorite hymns was "When I survey the wondrous cross." The whole things was so genuine that if people will confront it fairly and honestly, with a minimum of presupposition, they cannot remain the same.

We have already seen, in previous chapters, that Luke stresses Christ's prayers more than do the other writers. It is therefore no surprise to find that in his particular account, Christ's very first words on the cross were words of prayer: "Father, forgive them; for they know not what they do" (23:34). This prayer is striking for many reasons, the first being the fact that in spite of the physical agony and pain, it was a prayer for others rather than for Himself, and, above all, a prayer for those who caused His agony. Long before, as part of His teaching about prayer, He had said, "Pray for those who abuse you" (Luke 6:28), and now He could put His own command to the test.

The injunction to pray for enemies is a marvelous example of ethical concreteness. It is not very hard to assent to the abstract idea of loving one's enemies, but we have a complete escape from abstraction when we start to *pray* for them. Then we are doing something. And one of the natural results of praying for those whom we hate is that we begin to hate them less. If we pray for those who are cruel, we begin to "walk in their moccasins" and to see the world as through their eyes. If I could know all that is in the cruel man's heart, perhaps seeing some of the pain that has been a partial cause of his cruelty, I might be more tender in my judgment of him. At least I might begin to understand what Christ says in His first prayer on the cross, that the cruel man does not really understand what he is doing. It is conceivable that if he could know, if he could be aware of the harm he is doing, he would not do it.

Christ does not wholly subscribe to the Socratic paradox that vice is ignorance, but He comes very close to it. Whether all men would change if they were really to know the harsh consequences of their acts in the lives of other people, we cannot be certain, but Christ does assure us that His particular persecuters were unaware of the dire consequences of their act. They could not imagine how the pain of weight against pierced flesh would feel, and they could not, in their ignorance, know that they were bringing suffering and death to One who was, in the words of Colossians 1:15, "the image of the invisible God."

The importance of this prayer to early Christians is shown by the fact that it seems to have been deliberately imitated by Stephen in his martyrdom. The very last words of Stephen, as he died by stoning, were "Lord, do not hold this sin against them" (Acts 7:60). The picking up of the same note is not surprising when we realize that we are dealing with two volumes of the same general work. The fact that the prayer was employed by Stephen helps to strengthen the authenticity of the prayer in Luke, which does not appear in all manuscripts.

The more we contemplate, the less surprising it seems that the opening words of our Lord at the scene of His physical death should be words of forgiveness. We have already seen how central the concept of forgiveness is in the Pattern Prayer, which tells us that we need both to forgive and to be forgiven. On the cross, Christ was not telling how or for what we should pray, but was engaged in His own prayer. As the representative of His heavenly Father He was asking for the forgiveness of others and thus participating in the divine grace of forgiveness. Since His entire life, as well as His death, was a revelation of the character of the Father, the nature of the forgiving God was demonstrated dramatically on the cross.

The theme of forgiveness started early and continued throughout Christ's public life. Jesus first won the enmity of the religious leaders, not primarily by healing the paralytic, but by saying to him, "My son, your sins are forgiven" (Mark 2:5). The act of forgiveness was more offensive to the Pharisees than either the teaching or the healing, because it played havoc with the whole system of moral legalism. Naturally, the religious leaders, who saw in Christ's declaration of forgiveness a threat to everything they prized, accused Him of blasphemy.

We recognize something of the centrality of forgiveness in the Gospel when we face the fact that Chirst's Church is made up, not of the righteous, but of men and women who know that they are sinners. Christians are not people who are "good," but rather people who realize acutely that they are *not* good. Even Christ identified Himself with humanity by answering, when He was addressed as "Good Master," "Why do you call me good? No one is good but God alone" (Mark 10:18). We do not know all that this means, but it evidently seemed important to the first Christian writers, for Matthew and Luke corroborate the story (Matt. 19:16-17, Luke 18:18-19).

Not all Christians repeat the following words from the prayer of General Confession each time they meet: "We have left undone those things which we ought to have done; and we have done those things which we ought not to have done; and there is no health in us." But all who truly belong to Christ say repeatedly something like this in their inmost hearts. It is therefore obvious that one of our reasons for responding to the first prayer on the cross is the recognition that we are involved in it. In a sense He is praying for us! We participate in the crime of the crucifixion in every act of cruelty in which we engage. Once we know this, we are very glad to have Christ pray to the Father that we, in our ignorance, be forgiven. But there is one thing worse than the act of those who know not what they do. That is the act of those who know perfectly well what they are doing and go ahead, regardless of consequences to others. Did Christ also pray for such? We do not know.

Any discussion of divine forgiveness leads to a consideration of the atonement. This is a great mystery, and, though it has received the attention of some of the most thoughtful of men, it is still mysterious. At least, however, we can be sure that what occurred on the cross did not change God's character or His attitude toward His erring children. Instead, it demonstrated His character and attitude. Thus the mature expression of the atonement that we know was that of the Apostle Paul when he wrote, "God was in Christ reconciling the world to himself" (II Cor. 5:19). It is we who need to be reconciled to God, not God to us. Of this we can be sure, if, as the New Testament teaches, God is like Christ. "The cross of Christ is not the means of procuring forgiveness, the Father wants to be gracious."[4]

If Christ is the true revelation of the Father, as He said He was, then it follows that God is always *seeking* to forgive. He is reaching out to seek and to save, even to the uttermost. He stands at the door and knocks (Rev. 3:20). He is the "Prodigal Father," prodigal in His affectionate concern, and, in suffering love, seeking to induce the repentance which makes a new start possible. It is not merely that God offers a new start to those who repent. What if I don't *want* to repent? What if I *like* the wrong things I am doing? The experience of Christ on the cross, if I face it fairly, itself induces repentance and therefore makes the new start possible. When the new start comes, the past is really obliterated, so far as the love of God is concerned. The atonement undoubtedly means much more than this, but it means at least this much and the first prayer on the cross is an important part of our evidence. If God were not by nature forgiving, Christ could not have prayed, "Father forgive them." Dr. G. Ernest Thomas provides a summation in the sentence, "Christ's forgiveness uncovered the sympathetic heartbeat of Almighty God."[5]

We must beware, in this connection, of interpreting the divine forgiveness as a loose and easy tolerance. At the cross, we are miles away from the sentimental aphorism, "To understand all is to forgive all." The notion that God looks with kindly tolerance on all human acts, even when we seek to destroy the reputations of others for the sake of our own ad-

[4] Henry Sloane Coffin, *The Meaning of the Cross* (New York: Charles Scribner's Sons, 1931), p. 121.

[5] *Op. cit.*, p. 27.

vancement, is not a Christian idea, whatever it may be. The meaning of forgiveness is not that God as revealed by Christ overlooks indulgently all of our failures and constantly says "Never mind." Love so interpreted is not superior to the stern conception of Yahweh, with his moral plumbline (Amos 7:8), but vastly inferior to it. The forgiveness of God consists, not in being unmindful of sin or sentimentally tolerant of it, but mindful of it in a way that is redemptive. True love neither neglects sin nor merely condemns it, but finds a third and creative way of facing it. Caring goes beyond both tolerance and vindictiveness to a way which is truly redemptive. This is the way of the cross!

Every act of forgiveness entails a new start, and for one who seriously tries to be in Christ's company, every day is such a new start. Dean Coburn has put this persuasively as follows:

The key is in beginning again. Indeed it can be said from one point of view that this is what the Christian life is all about: *it is being willing to begin again.* So often we respond to God out of some deep experience and promise to lead a new life with his help. Then we forget his help and fail. This is the crucial point. We can give up in despair or we can begin again. It is the starting afresh patiently and in good cheer and hope that is the mark of the Christian. One of the helpful definitions of Christianity is this: the Christian life is a series of new beginnings.[6]

The second prayer on the cross is taken directly from the 22nd Psalm, its use on this occasion indicating a deep familiarity with the text. If we may judge from Christ's quotations, as it is reasonable to do, we conclude that His favorite books of Hebrew Scripture were Deuteronomy, Isaiah, and Psalms. That He drew on all three types of Hebrew literature is indicated by His words after the resurrection, "These are my words which I spoke to you, while I was still with you, that everything written about me in the law of Moses and the prophets and the psalms must be fulfilled" (Luke 24:44).

[6] *Prayer and Personal Religion, op. cit.,* p. 80.

In the temptations, the answer comes in every case from the words of Deuteronomy. The temptation to make bread is answered by Deuteronomy 8:3, the temptation to power by Deuteronomy 6:13, and the temptation to engage in spectacular acts by Deuteronomy 6:16. When Christ experienced His sad and crucial visit to the synagogue at Nazareth, He selected the noble passage in Isaiah 61:1-2. But in the supreme crisis of the crucifixion, He employed the spiritual resources of the Psalms, specifically 22 and 31.

There was good reason for Christ to be reminded of Psalm 22:18 as the executioners claimed His clothing as their right: "They part my garments among them, and cast lots upon my vesture" (AV). What had been metaphorical in the ancient literature became actual and literal in the crucifixion. Also, the scoffing and mocking of the chief priests, scribes, and elders would bring to mind another passage of Psalm 22, verses 7 and 8, as follows: "All they that see me laugh me to scorn: they shoot out the lip, they shake the head, saying, He trusted on the Lord that he would deliver him: let him deliver him" (AV).

Both of these passages would be reminders of the beginning of Psalm 22, which Christ used as His own anguished prayer, or what, sometimes, is called the prayer of dereliction, "My God, my God, why hast thou forsaken me?" For some reason Luke did not include this prayer, whereas Matthew follows Mark in retaining it. The use of the agonizing prayer has seemed shocking to some devout Christians, while it has been a boon to others. If we take the prayer straightforwardly, at its face value, the prayer represents a response, as does the prayer in Gethsemane, to a temporary testing so severe that it almost leads to despair.

If there was, on the cross, a brief time of despair, it is wholly understandable. The loneliness must have been almost unbearable. The crowd, instead of being moved to compassion by His suffering, were either idly curious or openly glad that He was in torment. Instead of compassion, which He needed at this point, He received ridicule. Many apparently thought that His claims had been too great, and now they were glad to see Him brought low. Prizing the temple as they did, they had resented His statement that if it were destroyed, He could rebuild it in three days. In their literal-mindedness they had missed the point of what He had said, and they did not understand His claim that "something greater than the temple is here." Now He could not save even His physical body. What, therefore, had become of His great pretensions?

The loneliness was accentuated by the cowardice of His followers. Where were the Twelve to whom He had given His closest attention? Where were the members of the innermost circle, once gathered for prayer on the Mountain of Transfiguration? Mark indicates that Christ's major response to this terrible aloneness was silence. In any case, His silences occupied much more time than His utterances. Mark presents Him silent for six full hours, i.e., from 9 A.M. to 3 P.M., and making His only utterance at the end of this long period. Apparently Mark did not know of the prayer for the forgiveness of the persecutors nor of the assurance given to the penitent thief. This provides a good illustration of the value of having more than one account, so that the records are balanced and mutually supplemented.

It is reasonably clear to us why, out of all possible references, Christ chose to use Isaiah 61 when He inaugurated His program at Nazareth, but why, on the cross, did He employ the anguished cry of Psalm 22? The other parts of the Psalm help us, but they do not provide a sufficient reason. Did the use of "My God, my God, why hast thou forsaken me?" mean that temporarily He felt forsaken, not merely by men, but also by His heavenly Father? Did it mean that the closeness of the relationship evidenced by the other prayers was at last dubious? What a paradox if at the time of the ultimate test, He began to doubt what He had been saying! Did the very experience which, in our subsequent reflection, makes men see Him as the supreme revelation of the Father, cause

Him then to cease, momentarily, to feel the reality of the divine relationship? These are questions which we, as mortals, cannot answer. We do not know! But what we do know is that His experience on the cross, including His sense of absolute abandonment, brings Him closer to us than does anything else in the entire experience.

The Christian is not one who has absolute evidence, but is, instead, one who is *persuaded* that nothing can separate him from the love of God in Christ Jesus our Lord (Rom. 8: 39). We belong to the fellowship of faith, but we likewise belong to the fellowship of the humble and the perplexed, because we see through a glass darkly rather than face to face. Infallibility of judgment is the one boon which is clearly denied to man in his essential finitude. In this predicament, Christ, especially as seen in His prayers both in the Garden of Gethsemane and on the cross, seems very close to us. Every humble man who suffers moments of perplexity and doubt, or even despair, can take heart because Christ, Himself, prayed, "My God, my God, why hast thou forsaken me?"

The final prayer of Christ on the cross, and in His earthly life, is the prayer of victorious acceptance of the divine will. If the middle prayer on the cross expresses perplexity, as it appears to do, the final prayer is our evidence that this perplexity was only temporary. The entire tragic event ends on a triumphant note which transcends all suffering, loneliness, and despair: "Father, into thy hands I commit my spirit!" (Luke 23:46). If there could be a more reassuring conclusion, we cannot imagine what it is.

The final prayer of our Lord is, like the one which immediately preceded it, an echo from the Psalms, specifically 31:5. How wonderful that this ancient prayer of commitment was part of Christ's spiritual resource, ready to be brought to the surface of consciousness when most needed! That the use of this prayer by Christ was well remembered by the early Church, before the Gospels were composed, is indicated by the fact that Stephen repeated it, as he also repeated the first of Christ's prayers on the cross, when he faced his own death. The major differences are that Stephen reversed the order of the prayers, that he shortened the prayer of commitment, and that he addressed his prayer directly to Christ, rather than to the Father.

There is no way in which we can exaggerate the importance of our Lord's final prayer. It brings the whole story to a conclusion by pulling all of the parts together. Here, after temptations, healings, misunderstood teaching, and multiple crises, is the solution of the strain and stress. That gifted and saintly man, Gaius Glenn Atkins, compared the final prayer to the end of a symphony. "It is," he said, "a song of triumphant trust like the finale of the 'Symphony Eroica' in which the motifs which have stormed and sighed together through the long movement find their reconciliation."[7]

It is no wonder that, according to the record of the Gospels, this was Christ's last word, apart from those of the resurrection narrative. If this is not the last word there is no word. It is wonderfully appropriate that His last utterance, before He died, should have been an utterance of commitment, and that it should have been in the form of a prayer. It was not didactic; it expressed the I-thou relationship, and is the ultimate statement of that relationship. His greatest call had been a call to commitment when He said, "Come to me—take my yoke upon you," and now He ended with His own commitment. Commitment, we must remember, is much more significant than mere belief. It includes belief, but the belief is transmuted and glorified when it is crossed with courage. Commitment, therefore, is a hybrid, with all the strength of a hybrid, plus fertility.

Commitment, because it is the final thing, is also the principal thing. A Christian is one who is committed to Jesus Christ in every way. Such commitment is the diametrical opposite of cool detachment, and for that reason it is always hazardous. Because commitment includes involvement and consequent

[7] *Op. cit.*, p. 58.

risk, it takes courage to care. The involvement always includes actions and not mere opinions. This is why the honest repetition of a creed is really a fearsome step. The words "I believe in God" do not mean "I incline to the opinion that in all probability there exists a Being who may not inappropriately be called God."[8] The words, if they mean anything at all, mean the determination to live and to act in the light of the declared conviction. It is to do what the Wright brothers did at Kitty Hawk. They did not merely voice the opinion that flight with a heavier-than-air machine was possible; *they got into the machine!* In so far as we have recovered in our generation the recognition that commitment is central to the Christian life, we are supported marvelously by the final prayer of our Lord.

Any honest consideration of the life of Jesus Christ is both shaking and humbling. Whence came such power? The chief way in which we can find a reasonable answer to this question is by a continued study of His prayers. His prayers are not the whole of His revelation, but they are elements apart from which the other elements cannot be understood. The few prayers do not constitute the *sufficient* condition for understanding Christ, but they do constitute a *necessary* condition. What was His secret? George Buttrick has put it with convincing brevity: "The open secret is: His days were steeped in prayer. The missing word is God, and only by prayer can we find it."[9]

When we try with all of our ineptitude to be Christians, we are committed, not to a system, but to a Person, and one of the facts which we know best about this Person is that He prayed. *His days were steeped in prayer.* And if our faith is warranted, He is still praying. The *Lord's Prayers* are not ended, for they are continuous (Heb. 7:25). It is "Christ Jesus, who died, yes, who was raised from the dead, who is at the right hand of God, who indeed intercedes for us" (Rom. 8:34). In the light of this truth, the final prayer is not really

[8] William Temple, *Christian Faith and Life, op. cit.*, p. 35.
[9] *Prayer, op. cit.*, p. 40.

final. We are called, individually and collectively, to continuous prayer, but, in this holy task, we are not alone, because nothing can separate us from the love of Christ. The last word for us, as for Matthew, is "And be assured, I am with you always, to the end of time" (NEB).

Scripture Index

127